CW01333772

The
Umbrella Murder

The young Markov in Bulgaria

The Umbrella Murder

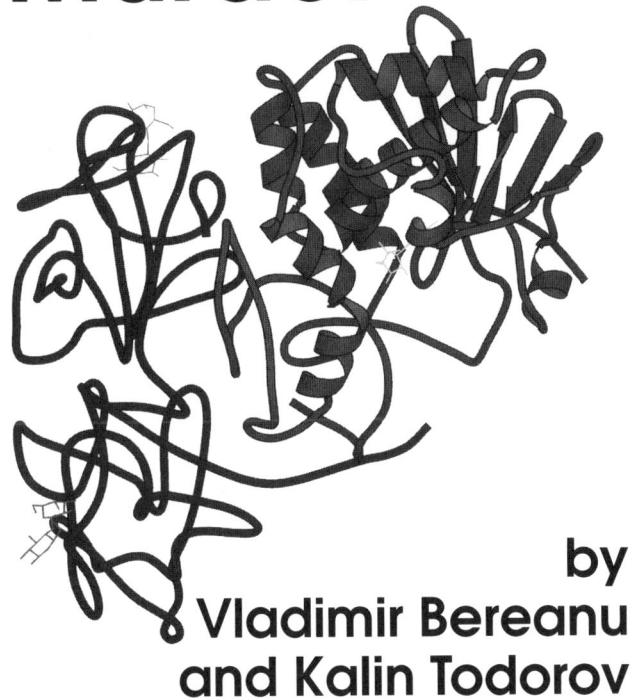

by
Vladimir Bereanu
and Kalin Todorov

First published in Bulgaria with the title
КОЙ УБИ ГЕОРГИ МАРКОВ?

Published by:
СИБИЯ

English translation and amendments: V Bereanu

First published in Great Britain, 1994
by T E L
St Andrews Castle
33 St Andrews Street South
Bury St Edmunds
Suffolk IP33 3PH

Copyright © T E L 1994

The authors assert the moral right to be
identified as the authors of this work.

Conditions of sale
All rights reserved. This book is sold subject to the condition that it shall not, by way of trade or otherwise, be lent, re-sold, hired out or otherwise circulated without the publisher's prior consent in any form of binding or cover other than that in which it is published and without a similar condition including this condition being imposed on the subsequent purchaser.

ISBN 0 9523573 0 5 Hardback

Designed and computer typeset by Sue Brettell

Set in New Century Schoolbook

Printed and bound in Great Britain by
Pendragon Press
Papworth Everard
Cambridge CB3 8RG

Cover design: Sue Brettell
Colour separations and map: Vicky Squires

Acknowledgements

Throughout the process of publishing this book, a steady stream of interest, suggestions and encouragement from professional acquaintances and friends has helped bring it to completion.

Tzveta Sofronieva's intense wish to see this book published – so that people in the West would be aware not only of Georgi Markov but also of the Bulgarian people's desire for honest reform – impressed me deeply. Aglika Markova and Donna Ireland have taken time to talk at length with me about Markov and the contemporary Bulgarian milieu. Late night discussions with Peter Moody (of the Protein Structure Research Group, University of York) led to contact with Professor Jon D Robertus (of the Clayton Foundation Biochemical Institute, University of Texas, Austin) who generously made available the photograph of the ricin molecule.

I am particularly indebted to Graeme Peene for his insistent encouragement at a time when there seemed to be more obstacles than solutions; to Andrew Millard and Stephen Badcock for believing in the book and in me; to Bill Barry for legal counsel, probing questions and intelligent comments; to Jeremy Beale for putting the question which helped focus the purpose of the book.

Sue Brettell joined the project with unreserved commitment and expertise, bringing with her ideas, contacts and an aesthetic technical precision which have subtly polished and refined the book. Roger Ellen and Brian Watt of Pendragon Press have been enthusiastic and helpful from the earliest discussions through to production.

I owe personal thanks to my friends, Mark Perkins, Kay Ellis and Stephanie Patoir, who have listened tirelessly, offering suggestions and cheering me on; to professional acquaintances who have offered their particular expertise at one time or another; and also to all those along the way who have chimed up, "Oh, do you mean *The Umbrella Murder?*", continually reminding me of just how truly interested the British public is in the unsolved murder of a Bulgarian dissident living in Britain.

I cannot adequately express my appreciation to my children, Gwyn and Dylan, for their loyalty and patience, living with me throughout the sometimes trying process of publishing a book.

And not least of all, to Vladimir and Kalin because they dared to pick up the pieces that lay on the ground and to write with care about the life and death of Georgi Markov.

Jane Tienne
Cambridge 1994

Contents

	Page
List of illustrations	1
Publisher's Introduction	3
Authors' Preface	7
Map	10
I The Game is Greater than Life	13
II Playing for High Stakes	24
III Dissident or Professional Player?	32
IV The Game in Other Places	47
V A Wilderness of Mirrors	60
VI Longer than the Legs of the Traitor	70
VII We Never Forgive Fugitives	74
Postscript	93
Appendix A	95
Appendices B and C	96
Appendix D	97
References	99
Index	101

Illustrations

Frontispiece: Young Markov in Bulgaria

Page 10: Map of Europe

1. Markov as a boy with his mother and brother, Nikola
2. Markov and his first wife Zdravka, witnessing the marriage of friends
3. Markov with Ormankov at a TB sanatorium at Bladaya
4. Markov and other writers and intellectuals with Zhivkov on a hunting expedition
5. Markov in Bulgaria
6. The wedding with Annabelle
7. Markov with his brother Nikola and wife Annabelle in England in 1975
8. Markov and Nikola in England
9. Markov with Annabelle and daughter Sasha
10. Markov with Sasha
11. Dr David Gall, head of toxicology lab at Porton Down
12. The ricin pellet that was removed from Markov's thigh
13. Fanciful cross-section of the "poison umbrella gun"
14. Vladimir Kostov, Bulgarian journalist and émigré
15. Oleg Kalugin, former major-general of the KGB
16. Kyril Panov, head of the Bulgarian Section of Radio Free Europe
17. Dimitar Stoyanov, former Bulgarian Minister for Internal Affairs
18. Vlado Todorov, high ranking officer in the Bulgarian KDS
19. Nikolai Knokhlov, KGB officer who specialised in political murder
20. Boris Arsov, Bulgarian immigrant murdered a short time before Markov
21. Vassilena Stolyova, one of a group murdered in Vienna
22. Jelyo Jelev, putting flowers on Markov's grave in Dorset

Jacket: Markov in his office in the Bulgarian Section of the BBC

Publisher's Introduction

In the course of readying *The Umbrella Murder* for publication, one sceptical British professional suggested to me that while this book was of obvious interest to Bulgarians it was not, in his opinion, likely to interest British readers. His words have stayed in my head, sometimes like a taunt and others like a spur, to clarify for myself – and for the British readers whom I consider to be both more caring and enquiring than his view would give credit to – why I so strongly believe in the importance of publishing this book.

The way in which I became involved with *The Umbrella Murder* is, on a personal level, sometimes as bizarre and intriguing as the story itself – one person's experience of innocent enthusiasm, commitment-cum-naïveté, deception and, ultimately, determination to see it through.

The original manuscript I worked on had been produced on a typewriter and copied on a machine that gave unequal results, and it had been written with intense urgency, first in Bulgarian and then translated into rough English. It was a somewhat awkward manuscript – a challenge heightened by the sinister trail of events it revealed.

What began for me as a task of the trade became, along the way, both an introduction to and a first course in modern Eastern European history. I am in no way a specialist, yet even so, working to bring this book to print has changed my awareness of the greater concept of "Europe" which currently clamours for recognition from all of us, everywhere. I will never again be able to turn a deaf ear to news of troubles in the Balkans or in any of the nations of the former Soviet Union. Two trips to Sofia to meet with the authors and discuss their book inevitably involved meeting their friends and family members and to seeing with my own eyes how resolute and cheerful even the Bulgarians are, in spite of the nightmarish economic woes which are causing so much hardship to the ordinary citizens because of Bulgaria's political isolation in this time of democratic reform.

Initially, this book is the account of the efforts of Vladimir Bereanu and Kalin Todorov to answer the question "Who killed Georgi Markov?" Writer, dissident and exile, Markov's cruel political murder caused considerable outcry but it was, nevertheless, allowed to slip into investigative limbo land and has thus remained "unsolved" since it happened sixteen years ago.

Had Markov been an ordinary private citizen, perhaps his murder would have been investigated very differently – as in the case of four people murdered on a yacht in the Caribbean in January 1994 – and, hopefully, the culprit would have been found, prosecuted and punished. Instead, as a political murder, much more is involved than the straightforward ethical concern of one man's unlawful death. When investigating a normal crime of any type – which has no political aspects – investigative talent and normal human feelings are required. On the other hand, a crime with political involvement puts the investigators in a difficult position because, in such a case, everyone has strong views one way or another. No matter how objective his efforts, the investigator is attacked by both sides. Ultimately, perhaps only a reader who is not in any personal way politically involved is the best judge.

Bereanu and Todorov, in spite of difficult circumstances, outright obstacles and the inevitably conflicting feelings of people who knew – or knew of – Markov, have sought not only the *who* but the *why* of this international crime. In the political arena the latter is not only the more elusive to identify but also the more crucial as its repercussions are felt everywhere.

There are those who for personal or other reasons would prefer that Bereanu and Todorov had not followed up the trail so inexplicably abandoned by the official investigating bodies, both in Bulgaria and in England. Many Bulgarians, however, have expressed the wish to have this book published, as a kind of symbolic clearing of the air which will contribute to the spirit of openness and honesty which they desire for their newly emerging democratic society.

Not only was Markov a well liked person, he was also a popular, successful and respected writer in Bulgaria. Following his defection to the West in 1969, he continued to hold his place in both the hearts and minds of his countrymen through his broadcasts over BBC World Service and Radio Free Europe. However, any honest investigation into his murder must face certain realities which may render the hero human. I believe it is of greater respect to the Bulgarian people – and thereby to Markov as a member of that community – to not retreat from the possibility of learning details of his life which would have remained his private concern but for the serious political issues involved.

Why should British readers be interested in *The Umbrella Murder*?

Because while taking the life and death of one man as its focus, *The Umbrella Murder* gives the average reader the chance to have a different perception of this nasty business which has been so popularised by spy thriller novels and films as to have almost been rendered "harmless" in our minds, quite like what the numbing effect of TV violence has done to the sensibilities of generations of children.

It is all there for anyone to see and read, the history of the details and intrigues of the various groups which, one by one, have collectively informed what we all loosely know now as the KGB. The problem is that the books are too long, the details too many, the names too long, too difficult to pronounce and impossible to remember for those of us who have not grown up in the Slavic sphere. The sheer complexity – the passion for layered intrigue, cover-up, under-cover operations, exposure, betrayal and purges; the grotesque sense of honour and loyalty adhered to by people who by any other description would simply be called gangsters, hoodlums and murderers (as in the case of the "super spy" Alexander Orlov) – overwhelms and drowns us by the excess of information available. Not surprisingly most of us, without even consciously deciding to, accept what we are told by our own governments – in the encapsulated form of contemporary news reporting – about these nefarious "foreign devils".

As if to remind us not only that Markov's murder has never been solved but also of the incessant, insidious worldwide presence of secret service organisations, throughout November 1993 there was a steady stream of newspaper and television coverage of the shuffling and renaming of the KGB. MI6 has been uncharacteristically much in the news, with public discussion about its activities and organisation. Mossad, irrespective of the courageous peace initiatives between the Israeli government and the PLO, answered the call for peace by savagely eliminating two high ranking Hamas leaders. Rumours of a coming tide of right-wing terrorist attacks are rife in South Africa. Even as the British government – in open and direct negotiations with the Irish government – was trying to promote its most ambitious initiative for peace in Northern Ireland, it was caught out in a horrific contradiction: it was revealed that from well back into the Thatcher years there had been a sequence of secret communications with the IRA.

And Oleg Kalugin, the sometimes KGB agent – who is now described in our press as a committed "reformer" and "democrat", and who is making a private fortune for himself by dealing in scrap metal – has regaled us with fascinating tales of the KGB's schemes to scientifically induce earthquakes to destabilise America, of an aborted attempt on the life of Nureyev, and of yet more versions of the murky circumstances surrounding the death of the much respected Bulgarian writer and dissident, Georgi Markov.

J Tienne
Cambridge
May 1994

Authors' Preface

When our book, *Who Killed Georgi Markov?* was published in Bulgaria in February 1991, it caused a small sensation. For the first time Bulgarians could read all the facts surrounding the notorious murder of their greatly admired, exiled dissident and writer, Georgi Markov. That book, the result of long and serious investigations, presented possible solutions to the mystery of who killed Markov on Waterloo Bridge in London, and why. Despite the controversial nature of the material we reported, the book was well received.

Clearly one of the organisations involved in the case was the Committee for State Security or, as it is known in Bulgaria, the KDS. Although it was supposed to have been disbanded since the political reforms of the 10th of November 1989, this organisation is still very powerful. That was one of the reasons why all of the state publishing houses refused to print our book, in spite of its being an obvious best seller. Therefore, we turned to a private publishing house, which immediately saw its chance and took up the book. Not surprisingly, after it appeared, the state book distribution companies refused to handle it, so it was mostly sold by street booksellers.

Since that time the world has changed rapidly. An unsuccessful coup in the Soviet Union in August 1991 precipitated the decline of world Communism and ultimately resulted in the demise of the Union of Soviet Socialist Russia. In the centre of Europe, war broke out and continues unabated and with indescribable savagery in the former Yugoslavia. In Bulgaria, on the other hand, the people are intent on establishing a democratic country.

The democratic reform movement has come after long years of foreign domination. Bulgaria was liberated from Ottoman

(Turkish) rule in 1886 as a result of the Russian-Turkish War. From then until the end of World War II Bulgaria was a monarchy under the imposed Saxe-Coburg-Gotha dynasty. After Hitler's downfall and the division of Europe at the Yalta, Teheran and Potsdam summits, Bulgaria fell into the Soviet sphere of influence and the royal family was ousted. After a lengthy period of nomadic exile, Simeon, the heir to the throne, together with the Queen Mother and his sister, Ioana, settled in Madrid. He continues to live there as a businessman of average calibre and still harbours some hope of being the king of Bulgaria.

For about a year following the abdication of the royal family, Bulgaria was ruled by regents. Then, as a result of the referendum of 1947, the country was declared a republic. The monarchists, who today represent about 18% of the population, continue to contest the referendum as it was held under Soviet pressure.

Immediately after the referendum, a communist dictatorship was established in Bulgaria and lasted until the 10th of November 1989. As a member of the Eastern Bloc it did not differ significantly from the other communist states created in Russia after 1917 and in Eastern Europe after 1944. Its main characteristics were a one-party system, lack of political pluralism and freedom of the press, pseudo-parliamentarianism, full ideological dictatorship over science and culture, full isolation from the values of Western civilisation, and full police control over the minds and personal life of the people.

Bulgaria was under Soviet control and that is why to a great extent the political, economic and social life was very similar to that in the Soviet Union. But in contrast to the other Eastern Bloc countries, due to historical, cultural and geographic factors, feeling against the Russians was low. Although dominated by the Soviets, the comparative flexibility of the Bulgarian regime managed to soften and block all attempts of resistance. That is why there is no trace of events in Bulgaria comparable to the Hungarian uprising in 1956, of the Prague Spring of 1968, or of the revolts in Poland which gave birth to "Solidarity". Furthermore, the information blackout used by the regime successfully blocked any popular outcry in support of these events in Bulgaria. There was hardly any information on the Hungarian uprising while the Czech events were subtly manipulated by propagandists and presented to the Bulgarian people as a counter revolution put down by progressive forces. Thus, only a small number of intellectuals – among them Georgi Markov – reacted and expressed a measure of protest.

Just as modern Bulgarian history has undergone many sweeping and rapid changes, events and facts around the Markov case have evolved at a similar pace, almost to the point of being difficult to follow. Even so, thanks to hard work and some luck, new facts have come to light and are published here. Some of these facts are not even known by either the Scotland Yard detectives investigating the case or by their Bulgarian counterparts. Consequently, and for obvious reasons, some of the people whom we believe to have been directly involved are referred to only by their code names.

The present edition is significantly different from the original published in Bulgaria. We have sought to clarify and more precisely define the issues surrounding Markov's murder, both by adding new information and by cutting back on unnecessary peripheral details. Most importantly, it contains the solution to the murder of Georgi Markov – as we have deduced it, in spite of the persistent and cunning efforts to obscure, confuse and even obliterate the plentiful facts.

We hope that we have been able to recreate a sense of the oppressive atmosphere of life under a Communist dictatorship such as the Bulgarian people have had to endure. While most Western readers have not personally experienced this kind of tyranny, hopefully they will sympathise with the many who do the world over. Perhaps greater awareness of the menace and of the insidious conditions which nurture it will help people to recognise and reject this oppression which, ultimately, goes so far as to deny the individual right to life and happiness.

We sincerely hope you will be moved by this book.

Vladimir Bereanu and Kalin Todorov
Sofia, Bulgaria 1994

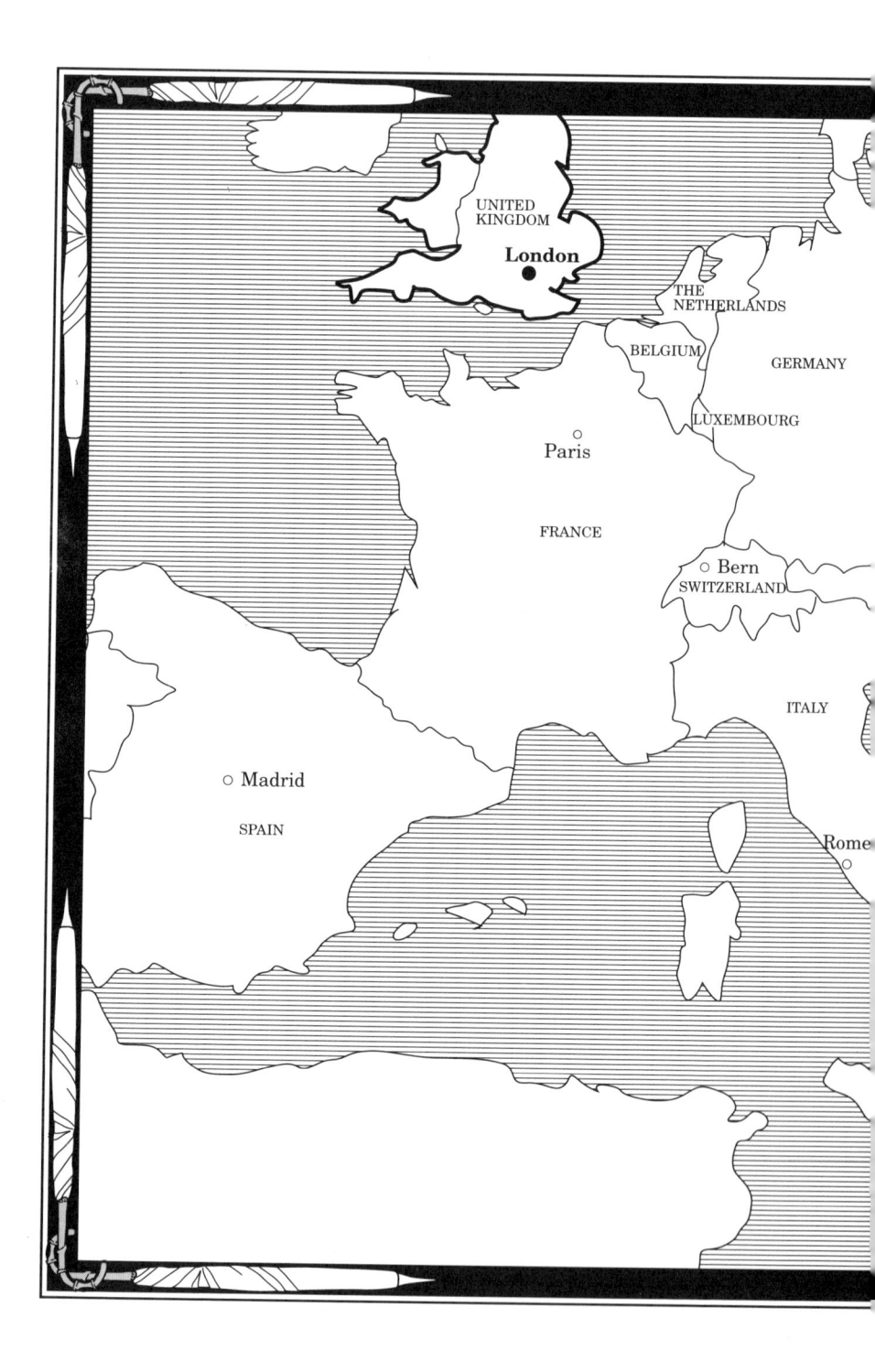

UNITED
KINGDOM
London
THE
NETHERLANDS
BELGIUM
GERMANY
LUXEMBOURG
Paris
FRANCE
Bern
SWITZERLAND
ITALY
Madrid
SPAIN
Rome

erlin
Warsaw
POLAND
RUSSIA
Kiev
Prague
CZECH REPUBLIC
SLOVAKIA
Vienna
AUSTRIA
Budapest
HUNGARY
ROMANIA
Bucharest
FORMER YUGOSLAVIA
BULGARIA
Sofia
ALBANIA
GREECE
TURKEY

Chapter I

The Game is Greater than Life

The 7th of September 1978 was a typical London day. The leaden clouds blanketed the city and seemed to hold everything in suspension. The usual colour and motion were there – signs on shops, bright green grass, blue-grey river, pedestrians weaving through the streams of buses and speeding cars along the riverside boulevard – but neither the flash of speed nor of colour could animate the gloomy surroundings or relieve the premonition of evil under the sun.

At a bus stop on Waterloo Bridge people calmly waited their turn while red double decker buses, full of passengers, came and went. Under the bridge, there is a metered parking place where many people leave their cars for the day while they work in the city. Nearby is the massive and sombre concrete bunker of Bush House, headquarters of the BBC "World Service". On that day, a few feet from the bus stop, a London cab was waiting patiently.

At about 3 pm a man came up the steps from the parking lot below the bridge. He always parked his car there. The distance to Bush House was only two stops by bus; sometimes he walked but he usually took the bus. From Waterloo Bridge anyone with knowledge of the man's daily routine could observe his arrival.

The man arrived at the bus stop and got into the queue. Suddenly he felt a sting in the back of his thigh, like that of a wasp. He turned in surprise and someone behind him said: "I'm sorry! I beg your pardon! Excuse me, please!" Later he could not remember the exact expression used by the man behind him, but what is certain is that the man had dropped his umbrella and as he picked it up, he excused himself in good English that had a slightly foreign accent.

The bus arrived. The man with the umbrella suddenly left the queue and got into the waiting cab. The cab took off and vanished. The face of the driver was never clearly seen. Our man got off the bus at Bush House and didn't return to his car for the next two hours. Thus ended a seemingly insignificant incident on Waterloo Bridge.

Settled in one of the studios at the BBC, the man adjusted the microphone in preparation for his 4:30 pm broadcast. He was the Bulgarian émigré, writer and broadcaster, Georgi Markov. He was about fifty years old. His best friend described him in this way:

> *He was of average height, thin and a casual dresser. He wore quality clothes, but he was not one of those close-shaven, well-pressed, well-shoeshined dandies that one often meets among his circle. Actually, he was the opposite. He looked as if he shaved after lunch. Without being handsome, he had an attractive face and he always had lots of success with women. He had exclusive charm. It was impossible not to become friends with him. Generous beyond his means, he always paid the bill. Just talking to him was a great experience and I have always been sorry for not writing down my discussions with him.*

What dark waves had brought this charming Bulgarian writer from the sleepy, dusty, provincial town of Sofia – his birthplace – to this cloudy, rainy island metropolis, steeped in its great past?

Before his broadcast, Georgi Markov asked Theo Lirkov (also a Bulgarian émigré) to examine the spot where he had been stung while waiting at the bus stop. Markov removed his trousers and indicated the place. Lirkov said he could see a small red dot, but neither of them thought the slight mark was important.

When the broadcast ended, Markov and Lirkov plunged into

the usual hour-long battle with London traffic, among the worst in Europe in spite of the excellent traffic police. It was well after 6 pm when Markov got to his house in South London.

From the noise and commotion of the city centre, he had returned to the almost rural calm of the suburbs with their endless rows of semi-detached houses and small garden plots, forming quiet streets where traffic is scarce. Only the coming and going of people of many nationalities reminds us that we are still in the capital.

Somewhere during the night, around 4 am – when Markov was wakened by his alarm clock for his early morning shift at the BBC – he felt ill and had a high temperature. His wife called another Bulgarian to stand in for him and she herself went to work.

Later, around 11 am, Markov answered his phone only after it had rung repeatedly and insistently. It was his brother, Nikola Markov, on the line. (Also an émigré since 1963, Nikola had first lived in Italy and later moved to Canada where he makes his living as a stamp dealer, catering for rich collectors.)

Georgi's voice was weak: "It's you, is it?"

"Yes, how are you?"

"I'm ill. I've got a fever and my doctor is away on holiday somewhere."

"How come you are ill? I hear the weather is warm and sunny, even in London. What have you been up to?"

"I don't know what's the matter with me."

Over the next hours all the normal home remedies proved futile as his temperature went on rising. Then, some while after his brother's call, the provincial calm of the street in south London was disturbed by the wail of an ambulance siren as it rushed the Bulgarian émigré to St. James' Hospital. He had lost consciousness and a team of doctors struggled for twenty-four hours to save his life. After the first crisis, he regained consciousness briefly and told his wife what had happened on Waterloo Bridge. However, by Monday the 11th of September he was still seriously ill and his condition suddenly worsened.

Markov's wife Annabelle recalled: "The next morning I got a

call from the hospital just as I was leaving home to go there, saying that Georgi's heart had started giving out in the night and that I should come in straight away. This I did, and as soon as I got there I realised for the first time that Georgi was dying. I could see it."

"I know that if someone is on the brink of death you can sometimes pull them back if they want to live – and Georgi did want to live, he never spoke of dying – if you can get to their subconscious ... so I was trying to get him to fight. I was saying: 'You have to fight for Sasha and me, you have to.'"

"Georgi said, 'Yes, Mama.' And then I saw the heart machine; I just saw it die away and I rushed out of the room and got a nurse and shortly after that he died."

Heart attack? Pneumonia? The symptoms were highly contradictory. The only certain fact discovered by the medical team was the small prick on Markov's upper thigh.

In the beginning the doctors accepted the version that the heart muscle had given up – heart failure. But by the time Georgi Markov – who had been born far away in Sofia, the capital of Bulgaria – was buried at Annabelle's family church in a Dorset village, there were plain clothes detectives from the anti-terrorist squad among the mourners. Someone was now convinced they were dealing with a political murder.

Nikola Markov said: "To my great surprise, in the beginning Scotland Yard accepted the death as natural. I disagreed sharply. Discussions with police representatives continued for two full days. Finally, late on the second day, the chief of MI5's anti-terrorist squad came and listened to the report made by his subordinates, and then heard what I had to say. I repeated everything I knew and the man told me very frankly: 'Mr. Markov, as of today we consider Georgi Markov's death as murder. I will try and find out who is responsible for this.'"

During the autopsy the investigators found a clue in Markov's thigh that convinced them that he had indeed been the victim of a unique political murder plot. At Scotland Yard's forensic laboratory, the then Chief Scientific Officer examined the minute metal object that had been found in Markov's thigh. Under a high powered microscope it was clear that the object was an extraordinarily sophisticated pellet, no bigger than a pin head.

It was made of a complex alloy, containing 90 percent platinum and ten percent iridium, a substance which is not rejected by the human organism. There were four tiny holes passing through the pellet which the forensic experts were convinced had contained an infinitesimally small amount of a lethally toxic poison, though they had no idea which. The pellet is now a permanent exhibit in Scotland Yard's Black Museum.

A few days after Markov's death another broadcaster in the Bulgarian section of the BBC died in strange and sudden circumstances. His name was Vladimir Simeonov and he was only thirty years old. His body was found at the bottom of the stairs in his house. Seemingly he had died from an accidental fall.

A careful investigation by Scotland Yard detectives could not detect any evidence of foul play and Simeonov's death was accepted as natural, in spite of the strange and suspicious circumstances. Two glasses were found in the sink that did not bear any finger prints, not even his. Traces of a bottle of alcohol were found on a table, but Simeonov was a teetotaller. He was found dead two days after having been questioned by Scotland Yard regarding Markov's death. He lived alone and did not have a telephone.

Therefore, it is possible that someone could have visited him, induced him to drink something with poison in it and left him to die. Some time later, the person could then have returned to remove the bottle and to wipe away the finger prints.

But what could have been the motive? One theory is that

Simeonov was the "fingerman" – the person who had pointed out Georgi Markov to the killer and had given him details of Markov's daily routine. This theory is supported by Theo Lirkov's statement that a week before Markov's murder Simeonov was very nervous, and that when he found out about Markov's death, he was visibly shocked and had started trembling.

Simeonov himself had an ironclad alibi as he had been away from London on that fatal day, but he probably knew more than he had told Scotland Yard.

Speculation strengthened that a secret assassination squad was, for the first time, using bacteriological warfare agents against civilians in Britain. Scotland Yard now made a highly unconventional move. Detectives called on the resources of the government's top secret Chemical and Microbiological Warfare Establishment at Porton Down in Wiltshire. (The scene of many anti-war demonstrations, it is one of the most controversial and sensitive places in Britain.)

The task of the poison experts at Porton Down was to establish exactly how Markov and Simeonov had died. In the toxicology department headed by Dr David Gall, they had to identify whether the men had been killed by a lethal virus or bacterium, a nerve gas, or a poison. After a series of complex experiments it emerged that the likeliest candidate was an exceedingly lethal derivative of the castor oil plant, called ricin.

Ricin had never before been used for murder in Britain and the toxicologists did not know exactly what its effects would be on a human being. According to Dr Gall it was necessary, therefore, to check the symptoms that ricin can produce in a larger animal and compare them with those of Georgi Markov.

For this purpose the specialists from Porton Down injected a pig with ricin. They even made their own record of the pig's heartbeat on an electrocardiograph. The pig rapidly developed an abnormal temperature; then the white cell count in its blood shot up dramatically. Later it developed a cardiac collapse. Its heart started beating extremely irregularly and it died not long after that. The complex picture was so similar to that of Markov that the experts from the laboratory excluded any possibility of coincidence.

Shortly before Markov's cardiac collapse occurred, his white cell count increased from eleven thousand to twenty-six thousand. A lethal dose of ricin for most species of animals that we know about, including Man, is about one microgram: difficult to put into lay terms, it is about a thousandth of a tiny pinch of salt per kilo of body weight. For a man who weighs about 70 kilos, the tiniest pinch could be a lethal dose.

According to the experts from Porton Down, it takes 70 times as much cyanide to kill a man. An ounce of ricin could kill 90,000 people. Furthermore, because the symptoms take a long time to develop, the murderer can be far away before suspicions are aroused.

However, the toxicologists investigating the Markov and Simeonov deaths found no ricin in the second dead Bulgarian and concluded he had died of a heart defect.

Another interesting discovery made at Porton Down is that the pellet found in Markov's body was probably sugar coated. As the sugar dissolves in the blood stream, the ricin is freed. On searching through an extensive medical bibliography, Dr Gall noted that one of the major papers on the toxicity of ricin – and a surprising proportion of the research into this subject – had been published in Hungary and Czechoslovakia. Not only is the castor oil plant widely grown in these countries, but there is also considerable interest in the toxicity of ricin.

Now Scotland Yard had to clarify another question. How had the pellet found its way into Markov's thigh? No traces of gun powder or other explosives were found on the pellet, which led the investigators to the conclusion that the pellet had been shot through a compressed air device, maybe an air pistol. The agent must have been the man behind Georgi Markov at the bus stop – the man who picked up his umbrella, the man with the slight foreign accent – and he, according to the British police, was the physical murderer.

Immediately after the murder of Markov, Scotland Yard put a blanket of secrecy over the investigation. The explanation was that any publicity would allow the organisers of the crime to hide clues and manufacture false evidence. Hence, the only story that did come out was Markov's own account (given when he briefly regained consciousness) of the incident at the bus stop, which gave rise to the story of the famous "Bulgarian umbrella".

Giant headlines covered the front pages of *The Times, The Observer, The Guardian, Corriere della Serra, Le Monde, and The Washington Post:* "Stay Away From Bulgarian Umbrellas", "The Murderous Umbrella", and "Poison Dart Shot From An Umbrella". A large shop selling umbrellas in Paris put a sign in its window saying "Sale of umbrellas to Bulgarians prohibited." Unfortunate Bulgarian visitors to the West got soaked whenever it rained, and those who had umbrellas hid them under their raincoats. As we will see, however, the whole umbrella myth was a colourful journalistic invention.

What is more, the umbrella is not the only journalistic invention in accounts about Markov's murder. After his death and as a result of Scotland Yard's silence, many "journalists" leapt at the chance to use their imagination. We won't mention all the different devices concocted by various writers as Markov's murder weapon, but the one created by *The London Evening Standard* in 1979 is worth commenting on.

Their big headline said: "Markov Killed By 'Cancer Gun'." The article went on to describe a "cancer" pistol with a magazine containing 14 small radioactive gold pellets with a length of 2.5 mm and a diameter of 0.8 mm. There is even an x-ray picture of such an implanted pellet in a human body which is supposed to have caused cancer of the liver.

How did the journalist from *The London Evening Standard* come up with such an ingenious idea? Perhaps he had visited Bulgaria as a tourist at some time during the Communist regime. During those years, menus in many big Bulgarian restaurants started with a "crab cocktail". In Bulgarian, however, there is one word for both *crab* and *cancer,* and so, because of an incorrect translation, Bulgarian menus often proudly began with something called a "cancer cocktail". Therefore, it could be assumed natural that people who offer cancer cocktails for openers would kill off their enemies with "cancer guns".

Ten days before the shooting of Markov in London, an assassination attempt had been made against another Bulgarian émigré, Vladimir Kostov, at a Paris metro station.

Kostov had been a popular journalist and political commentator in Bulgaria, working for Bulgarian Radio and newspapers like *Otechestven Vestnik, Anteni* and the Bulgarian Communist Party newspaper *Rabotnichesko Delo.* The Party newspaper sent him as its correspondent to Paris, where he led a double life of journalism and spying. Kostov readily admits now to having been a colonel in the Bulgarian KDS.

Then, after some years of service as a political agent, Kostov decided to ask for political asylum in France (towards the end of his term as Paris correspondent). His explanation for this change of heart was that the Bulgarian Communist government was undermining the country's sovereignty and independence by subordinating national interests to those of the Soviet Union.

Like Markov, after his defection he started working for Radio Free Europe. Then, ten days before the Markov shooting, as Kostov and his wife emerged from one of the Paris metro stations, Kostov felt a sting in the back, like the "wasp" sting which ten days later would strike Markov on the other side of the Channel. The couple turned around and saw a man disappearing in the crowd. In Natalya Kostov's words: "He was a very nondescript person and he did not have an umbrella."

Vladimir Kostov recalled: "The man had a small bag which could have held a few things but not an umbrella."

Although Kostov had a fever with a dangerously high temperature for three days, he managed to survive. Later, after hearing about Markov's death and the strange circumstances surrounding it, he had his back x-rayed. Close examination revealed a tiny metal object. A macabre dialogue with the French police ensued before the two Scotland Yard detectives arrived at Les Bluets Clinique in Paris.

There, under the eye of a French police inspector who wore a surgical mask and gown, Kostov was operated on. Later, Kostov described the procedure: "The surgeon had to be extremely careful: he removed the metal pellet without touching it at all, and to do that he had to cut away a piece of my flesh about three to four centimetres in size. They then x-rayed it to check that the pellet was still in the flesh. The whole thing was handed over to one of the Scotland Yard inspectors who took it back to England straightaway for analysis."

Using a high-powered scanning electron microscope, Scotland Yard metallurgists analysed the pellet taken from Kostov's back. Anti-terrorist squad detectives crowding round the microscope learnt that the pellet was identical to the one found in Markov. Both pellets weighed exactly the same, the holes were in the same places and both were made of a rare platinum iridium alloy that the human body does not reject. So sophisticated was the pellet that Scotland Yard was now convinced it must have been manufactured by the secret service organisation of a political state.

This information naturally leads one to ask why Kostov had survived when Markov suffered so horribly and died.

Although the blood sample taken from Kostov's body was discovered to contain ricin antibodies, the medical experts determined that the Kostov pellet must have been damaged before or during the shot. Because of bad transportation or some other reason, the pellet's sugar coating had fallen or cracked, and it was therefore empty or contained very little ricin. What little ricin was left caused symptoms similar to those of Markov but had not been sufficient to kill.

What would the extravagant Hercule Poirot or the upright, provincial Miss Marple say to all this? A Bulgarian émigré writer working for Radio Free Europe dies mysteriously in London. A strange pellet is found in his body and death is probably caused by a rare poison called ricin. A second émigré – also a Bulgarian writer, also working for Radio Free Europe – lives through a similar experience in Paris, apparently thanks to Luck. We are sure that Agatha Christie's famous detectives would come to the same conclusions as Scotland Yard in this case: suicide was out of the question, so it had to have been murder.

The pellets were identical and so, probably, was the weapon – some kind of air pistol – so the motive and the murderer were likely the same in both cases. The unusual circumstances ruled out what detectives call the usual motives for murder – greed, sex, jealousy, revenge or money. Scotland Yard came to the conclusion that they had a political murder on their hands. The complex technology used in the murder excluded amateur, non-professional or terrorist organisations. There was only one possibility left: Scotland Yard's opponent had to be a recognised and powerful political state and its secret services.

What did the two Bulgarians have in common beside their nationality and the fact that both were literary men? Significantly, both were working for Radio Free Europe.

Chapter II
Playing for High Stakes

Georgi Markov had an unconventional career while he lived in Britain. He managed to work not just for the BBC's External Services (which is proud of its reputation for impartiality), but also for another radio station with a tradition very different from that of Bush House – Radio Free Europe.

These days Radio Free Europe likes to forget the image it used to project when it was founded by the Americans at the height of the Cold War in the Fifties. In 1971 it was revealed that much of the funding used to set up and run RFE had come from the CIA. Today they claim that all has changed: the station is now funded by the American Congress.

Markov used to broadcast weekly stories about life at the top in Bulgaria as part of RFE's daily output in six languages to Communist countries. One of the questions facing the investigators was whether Markov's and Kostov's work for RFE constituted sufficient motive for murder by the Bulgarian secret services.

It is clear that behind the plot stood an entire organisation. This theory was supported by the laboratory produced pellets, by the presence of the rare poison, ricin, by the use of a professional air propulsion device, and by the mysterious cab which took away the "man with the umbrella". Concerning this last point, Scotland Yard has an excellent relationship with cab drivers who very often help the police in their investigations, but in this case no cabbies answered the repeated calls by the police for information.

Even though the evidence pointed strongly to a political murder, the investigators researched all other possibilities as well. By the process of elimination, the detectives checked all Bulgarian immigrants, in order to exclude non political disputes as a motive for the murder. (Anyway, such an explanation would not fit the attempt on Kostov's life.)

The next step in the investigation was to consider the question of all official and unofficial personnel in the Bulgarian Embassy and other Bulgarian missions in Britain. After scrupulous investigation, Scotland Yard concluded that none of the Bulgarians living – either permanently or temporarily – in Britain had committed the murder. This led Scotland Yard to its second clear and categorical conclusion: the man who killed Georgi Markov must have been sent specially for this task from abroad.

Next came the tedious but necessary job of checking and comparing all possible incoming flights, lists of passengers and airline timetables. The investigators' guiding theory was that the murderer had come and gone from Great Britain by aeroplane, using a diplomatic passport in order to pass through customs control with his lethal equipment. If the murder had been organised by the secret services of a foreign power, it is clear that the passport had either been issued by that country or that a professional counterfeit had been obtained.

If the police were right, the murderer did not know Markov personally and so he needed the help of someone who knew Markov's habits and daily routine. According to MI5, this would have been an implanted agent of a foreign power in the BBC. The best candidate for this role was the other Bulgarian broadcaster, Vladimir Simeonov.

The mythical "foreign power" was, of course, the Bulgarian secret services. This speculation is made more plausible because of the fact that, before his death, Georgi Markov briefly regained consciousness and told of a man who had tried to warn him about an imminent attempt on his life – this had been only three days before the fatal encounter on Waterloo Bridge.

Georgi's brother, Nikola, had more to tell about the man who tried to warn his brother of the danger he was in. "In January

1978 a man called me – you can understand why I can't mention his name – and he told me: 'Kolyo, you have to hear something very important. In Sofia they have decided to bump off your brother. Do something about it! Warn him, at least, so he will take measures to protect himself. What actions they will take, how they plan to kill him, I don't know, but the decision has been taken! Please warn him to take great care, and to stay away from other Bulgarian émigrés, because you never know whom they serve and in what they believe.'"

"I called my brother immediately and told him what I had heard. He was a little surprised and answered: 'I don't believe they will dare to do it. If they do there will be such a scandal, they won't know what hit them.'"

"The months of February, March and April passed without incident and no new warnings. My brother worried less and during one conversation he told me: 'It's someone's idea of a bad joke; maybe they are trying to scare me.'"

"We often talked on the phone, in a brotherly way . . . In June my brother went on holiday to Sardinia. On the day of his arrival – if I am not mistaken it was the third or fourth of June – the same man called me and asked: 'Kolyo, where is your brother?' 'Why?' I asked him. 'Find him immediately! I'll tell you what is going to happen. Listen, the plan is this. In Sardinia he will, by chance, meet an old friend. I don't know who the friend is. This person will invite Georgi to a bar for a drink. At the friend's suggestion they will sit at the bar rather than at a table. While having their drink, Georgi will be called away by a phone call. During his absence the 'friend' will pour something in Georgi's glass – a very strong poison which leaves no trace in the bloodstream. The doctors will think he died of a heart attack. Tell him to talk to no one, not to accept drinks and to take good care. Keep in touch with me.'"

"After putting down the phone I immediately called England but there was no answer. I called the hotel in Sardinia and they told me the English group was to arrive around six or seven in the evening. I told them there was a very important message for Georgi Markov and that he should call me as soon as he arrived.

I called again around seven and talked to Georgi."

"He received the news seriously and started questioning me: 'Who told you all this?' I told him it was not important who told me, but that it should be taken seriously. Although Georgi usually never took anybody's advice, this time he took mine. He was always an individualist."

Nikola went on: "On the 17th of June I received a call from Bulgaria. Our father had died. I called Georgi at the hotel again and he received the news badly, really badly, even though our father had been very ill for more than a year; there was no hope for him and his death was expected. My brother went back to England and our phone conversations continued with greater frequency, once or even twice a week. I reminded him every time of the ominous warnings and finally I arrived in London on the third of August. I came personally to give him the latest information which I had received. It was very frightening. My friend had told me: 'Kolyo, very soon they'll try to kill your brother. In a very unusual way. I don't know how and I don't know when.'"

What happened to the plan to murder Markov in Sardinia? Had an attempt even been made? Nikola explained: "Georgi's and my explanation was that no attempt had been made because of the special security features at the resort where he spent his vacation. It was not a hotel, but a private residence with fenced off grounds. To enter it a person needed a pass. As a precaution, Georgi did not leave the compound which had its own beach, swimming pool and everything else. Even so, Georgi was never fully convinced of the danger, and he never fully believed in the warnings. He wanted practical proof. He never showed any open apprehension and he became careless after returning to London, especially since he stopped writing his reports for Radio Free Europe after our father's death."

Nikola continued to worry about his brother's safety: "During my visit to London in August we were together every day and we often discussed the warnings. I saw him for the last time on the 18th of August, at the airport. He went to buy some chocolate for my son and on his return I warned him for the last time: 'Gosho, take good care. Don't have anything to do with Bulgarians, it's too risky. You would never know who to trust!'"

"He answered crossly: 'Stop this. I'm fed up. If they want to kill me, let them kill me. I don't care.' These were his last words to me in connection with the attempt which was being prepared against him."

"I can't tell you who the man is – the one who gave me the warnings. If I did it would endanger his life. He is a Bulgarian, he knew Georgi well and was his friend. He was someone high up, someone important. But what I don't know is whether he himself was a party to the conspiracy or whether someone else had passed the information on to him. In any event, the most worrying warning came when he said that some sort of poison or bacterium – he didn't know exactly which – had already been brought out to Western Europe and was being stored in the Bulgarian embassy in one capital and in the Bulgarian consulate of another large western city."

Markov's wife, Annabelle, had also met this man: "The man first contacted Georgi at the very end of May, at the BBC. Then, he visited us at home and he and Georgi spoke Bulgarian the whole evening. Every so often Georgi would come to me and say in English: 'It's extraordinary what this man is saying.'"

"The man said Georgi would be killed for what he was writing for Radio Free Europe. He did not say who was actually going to do it, but he said that a decision had been taken at the highest level in Bulgaria, by the Praesidium or Politburo."

In spite of all the warnings and the very real concern of his brother, Markov still did not seem to be anxious for his safety. About this time, he was making plans to quit broadcasting altogether and to set up as a small, independent publisher working with other European writers, based in Paris. He had spoken of these plans to close friends and was looking forward to breaking from the activities which still linked him to the past. Perhaps the prospect of this contributed to his not taking the warnings seriously.

Today the man who tried to warn Markov is probably one of the few who, first hand, has the key to the question: "Who killed Georgi Markov?" He also emigrated from Bulgaria a few years ago. He is alive and in good health, living in Munich, Germany. He still thinks that if his name were published his life would be in danger.

We contacted this man three times and on each occasion he gave us a different version of what happened. During our first meeting he said that he had heard about the case "in the corridors of power"; the second time, that "friends in the highest echelons of power had told him". The third time he called us to say he was prepared to talk, only to change his mind later.

His behaviour is difficult to explain if we adopt the most popular theory on the Markov murder. According to this theory, Markov was murdered by the Bulgarian secret services on the orders of the Bulgarian dictator, Todor Zhivkov, who was incensed by Markov's reports about him which were broadcast on Radio Free Europe. The same reason is given for the attempt on Vladimir Kostov's life. But if this is so, why does the "man from Munich" still keep silent? The Bulgarian political situation has changed dramatically. Zhivkov was arrested and put on trial in Bulgaria, and he no longer figures as a serious political figure there. This theory is widely held by the press and presents no danger to anybody who supports it with the accepted "facts".

However, we maintain that the opposite is true: while there appears to be a tacit agreement by all sides to support this theory, is it the truth? In the interest of impartiality and in order to get to the truth, our book presents the different theories about Markov's murder, as well as offering our own solution because the perpetrators of this crime and the nature of their motive must be exposed. The evolving social and political situation in the former Soviet Union and its satellite nations should not lull us into thinking that all danger is past. The "man from Munich" knows that there is still good reason for keeping silent and for guarding his identity.

In 1979, Scotland Yard turned to the counter intelligence department of MI5 for help. This was natural as most of the facts pointed to secret Bulgarian participation. True to its reputation, MI5 came up with a photograph and a name – that of a Bulgarian diplomat who had arrived at Heathrow airport in time for the murder and had left immediately after it was committed. MI5 discovered that he was travelling under an assumed name, different from the one he used as a Bulgarian diplomat in a West European country. He had a diplomatic passport and so his luggage was immune to customs checks.

Here Scotland Yard came to a dead end. What had started on Waterloo Bridge as a typical detective novel murder came logically to the stage where the sleuths would have to investigate in that unknown land, Bulgaria. The Bulgarian authorities offered their help, but there had to be something wrong when the main suspect offers to cooperate in the investigation against him. Thus, the British authorities declined the "help" offered by the Bulgarian Communist regime, fearing that such cooperation would only help the Bulgarians to destroy any existing clues. The "Georgi Markov Murder" file went into the Scotland Yard safe, waiting for more auspicious times.

Finally, after a twelve year delay and in the aftermath of Zhivkov's fall from power, the Bulgarian State Prosecutor's Office ordered a full investigation into the death of Georgi Markov. It began on the 19th of October 1990, and this time the British authorities and Scotland Yard agreed to receive two Bulgarian investigators in London.

Though the purpose of their visit to London was serious, it was not on the cards that they would learn much. We talked to one of the two Bulgarians. According to him, Scotland Yard was still unconvinced of the nature of the political changes in Bulgaria and, though the two Bulgarian investigators were shown an excellent time (lots of sightseeing and good meals), they left London without any information or evidence on the Markov case.

Strangely enough, at this stage of the investigation we had

more information on the murder than the official Bulgarian investigators. We had published a few articles in the Bulgarian press which aroused considerable interest among readers who otherwise knew very little about the case. As a result, we were called upon by the investigators to give what evidence or information we had to them. This is how we came to be closeted with one of them in his small office on the fifth floor of the Central Investigative Office in Sofia.

The investigator, Mr Karayotov, an intelligent but tired man of about forty-five, had chased murderers for 25 years. He was clearly a good homicide detective but, given the nature and circumstances of Markov's murder, full prosecution of this crime was beyond his investigative means. He told us there was no money for an investigation which required the questioning of witnesses in England, Germany, Italy and Austria; that it was very hard to investigate the investigators, because if this was a political murder, then his colleagues from the secret service were probably involved, and so on.

We in turn told him all we knew about the man we suspected of having killed Markov – whom we had dubbed "Woodpecker". We shared other information we had with him in the sincere hope that he would solve the case and that the perpetrators would be tried. But coming out of his office we felt glum and admitted to each other that we did not think this man would ever get to the truth.

Before leaving his office we had managed to see a copy of the composite picture made by the French police as a result of the testimony of the other Bulgarian victim, Vladimir Kostov. The similarity between the man in this picture and what we knew Woodpecker to look like was striking although their man's hair was straight, while the man in our picture had curly hair.

Chapter III
Dissident or Professional Player?

Before elaborating on the strange unravelling of events in our investigations, and before trying to answer the question, "Who killed Georgi Markov?" we should try to answer the prior and equally important question, "Who *was* Georgi Markov?"

Markov was born in Sofia in 1929, the son of an army officer. Growing up during the tumultuous pre-World War II years profoundly affected the development of his personality. He attended the polytechnic university in Sofia and graduated as an industrial chemist. While a student he was imprisoned for a short time by the Communist authorities, as part of the "witch hunt" principle which believed that if you had any distant relation who had been a policeman, or an officer in the army, or even just someone with his own private business, you were potentially an "enemy of the people".

This experience, together with his natural tendency to "get on in society", inclined Markov to ingratiate himself with the system. According to many of his friends he was two persons in one man. The familiar Georgi Markov was a writer and dissident – a talented, sensitive person who hated the totalitarian Communist system and its aim of making everybody a non-person.

His first literary bestseller in Bulgaria, the novel *Men* was published in 1962. Then, as in a fairy tale, from that moment on, his successes came one after another. His books *Doctor Gospodov's Sanatorium, The Women of Warsaw, A Portrait of My Double,* the play *To Squeeze Through a Rainbow,* his film scripts and especially his TV series, *We Are at Every Kilometre* made him the best known contemporary Bulgarian writer. Quite naturally, he became a member of the "circle of power", the highest echelon in Bulgarian society. But this was not all.

One of Markov's best friends, HD, remembers him from this period: "We often discussed the situation in the country and we always came to the conclusion that changes were decided on by the big powers – changes about which the Bulgarian people were never asked – and we would be in this situation as long as the Soviet Bloc existed. We never believed Bulgaria would bloom under the flag of Communism. We were patriots, but we never believed in the so called 'bright future'."

"Although the police were not yet as repressive as they would become after crushing 'The Prague Spring' in 1968, we had already had the experience of Hungary in 1956. It was clear to us that no change was possible in the foreseeable future and so our motto was: 'Every man for himself'."

There is something rebellious in each of Markov's twelve applauded and successful plays and books, from the feverish confessions of the card-playing journalist in *A Portrait of My Double,* to the self-humiliation and disgust in *The Empty Space,* to the unbelievable and murderous beauty of *The Women of Warsaw.*

In one of the few recordings made by Markov in English he says of himself: "I tried to compromise as much as I could, and eventually it was too much. The whole atmosphere in Bulgaria was deeply contrary to my beliefs. I do not mean that I am, let's say, braver or more honest than other people. Perhaps if I were more honest I would still be there, because if you are honest you stay and fight for what is needed, there – not from here. I feel compelled to rebel against authority. If you really want to make me hate something, tell me that the authorities have decided how things must be, or worse, that they have imposed their will on me . . . that I could never, never accept."

After his defection to Great Britain Markov worked in the Bulgarian Language Department of the BBC, and actively collaborated with the radio stations Radio Free Europe and Deutsche Welle. He used to broadcast weekly reports about life at the top in Bulgaria as part of his work for the station. One of the most widely held theories is that Markov was murdered because of his work for Radio Free Europe. People say that Todor Zhivkov was infuriated by the portrait of himself presented in Markov's reports.

Zhivkov was probably the most grotesque and colourful figure among the dictators of Eastern Europe. He came to the pinnacle of power as First and then General Secretary of the Central Committee of the Bulgarian Communist Party, Chairman of the Council of Ministers, and later President, thanks to the struggle between two rival factions in the Party. Typical of such situations, the temporary compromise candidate took care of all his opponents and stayed in power for more than thirty years. (Nicolae Ceausescu was a very similar example.)

A crafty and cunning peasant, Zhivkov soon grasped a few elementary postulates which he applied successfully and which saw him through the eras of Khrushchev, Brezhnev, Chernenko and Andropov. He understood clearly that none of the East European countries could have either an independent foreign or internal policy and so he never contradicted the Russians on any question. There are even documents which show that he offered Brezhnev the inclusion of Bulgaria in the USSR as an independent republic.

The second basic truth which Zhivkov understood is that you should not destroy your opponents but buy them – otherwise, they become martyrs. For this reason, not only did he bestow honours on his eventual political opponents but also lavish sums of money and lots of privileges, and thus Bulgaria never had a political and intellectual opposition in the real sense.

Another of Zhivkov's "feats" was that he sold Bulgaria and its independence for guaranteed markets in the USSR and for access to enormous quantities of raw materials coming from the "Big Brother". Because of this, although the Bulgarian economy kept sinking there was no apparent hardship in the country.

Zhivkov managed to be a Bulgarian Machiavelli until Gorbachev and the times of "Glasnost" and "Perestroyka" when, seeing his end, he opposed the Russian leader at every step.

However, the undercurrent of change was too deep, even for him, and on the 10th of November 1989 his ex-cronies organised a palace coup and Zhivkov fell from power.

Later, Egor Yakovlev, one of the closest people to Gorbachev and his idiological genius, admitted that the Kremlin knew all about the intended coup and directed it. The aim was to change the leader while keeping control of the Bulgarian Communist Party and maintaining the close relationship between Bulgaria and the USSR. But the events which overtook the whole of Eastern Europe changed Zhivkov from an unchangeable leader to a criminal under investigation and on trial.

The trials have ended and Zhivkov has been sentenced to seven years in prison, mainly for spending millions of US dollars in helping left-wing movements all over the world. This money was obtained through arms dealing and facilitating the flow of drugs from the East to the West. That was one of the reasons why the CIA staged the so-called "Bulgarian connection" in the case of the attempted assassination of Pope John Paul II. The idea was to frighten off the arms and drug customers. It was a successful operation but the details of it are another story.

Whatever Zhivkov's crimes, it is doubtful if imprisoning an old man is the correct way to act in a civilised society. Many believe that he should be allowed to die of old age – as did the system he so wholeheartedly supported – not dissimilarly to Nixon in the United States. The ex-Communist Party is still the strongest political force in Bulgaria and popular support continues to consider the old regime as something better than the new "democratic" system which leaves people in impossible economic conditions and leads to massive unrest. To those who want freedom, this appears to be change, but for the others it is chaos. This is Zhivkov's legacy to contemporary Bulgaria.

How was Zhivkov presented in Markov's reports? Following are some excerpts:

The back door opened and I saw the face I knew from so many portraits and from the few rare meetings with the first man in the country. He was dressed simply in a casual jacket and cap – very like one of those old army uniforms. "Come on Georgi!

You're the last. We've been waiting for you!" he said full of goodwill and waved me to my place in the car with the experienced gesture of a good host.

From close up Zhivkov's face looked more symmetrical and maybe more inspired. In any case, it was a lively face with a careful self-assurance which did not irritate. His eyes gave the impression of energy and the power of observation. He was a person who could listen. In comparison with all the other members of the Politburo and most ministers, Todor Zhivkov was, in my opinion, the only one who knew how to listen without interrupting, without commenting, without giving his own opinions. This quality of his was very predisposing and that is why he is also the most deceptive.

The second thing I discovered while the "Chaika" (insiders' name for Zhivkov) was driving on the road to Vitinya, was his quality of directness and naturalness. For me personally it is very hard to be friendly with people I have just met, but in the car I had the well defined feeling of having known Zhivkov well and for a long time. I think this was not so much due to his acting in a purposeful manner but rather to his peasant background, to his farmer's blood. If you didn't know who he was and you met him without his bodyguards and entourage, you would think he was a village teacher or a postman or the local agronomist.

He looked very open and honest, and treated everyone as his equal, without making any effort to present himself as something he was not. All this strongly contradicted what I had seen of Zhivkov at the rostrum when making a speech. There, he seemed distant and most people thought of him as a remote and superficial speaker. What really angered me about his speeches was this low quality populist pathos which seemed compulsory for all political speakers in Socialist Bulgaria.

Listening to him, I recalled an earlier speech he made in 1963 when he called all the members of the Union of Artistic Professions together in the building of the Communist Party Headquarters and harangued us on the evils of divergence from the party line. On that occasion he demonstrated a distastefully mediocre humour while at the same time threatening us like a village policeman. He attacked all modern tendencies in Bulgarian literature, and accused us of following frivolous foreign fads, repeating over and over that we were to promote the everyday interests of the party.

The most offensive part of this clichéd and wearying speech was its tone, which revealed a disturbing lack on Zhivkov's part of any understanding of complex events. He compensates for this with the impudence of a not very intelligent petty dictator trying to command intellectual spirits whom he could neither fathom nor communicate with.

He came out of nowhere: his whole biography as the leader of the Bulgarian National Revolution was fabricated later. In the beginning people thought he was a temporary phenomenon. Following Stalin's death, when the changes of 1956 started and were connected to Zhivkov's name, no one – either on the left or on the right – took him seriously.

Both Stalinists and hard-liners openly made fun of him, while the people with more common sense were suspicious of him and did not believe him. Rumours of his imminent removal were rife. But the way in which he managed to eliminate his direct opponents and to overcome any obstacles to his power showed that the opinions people held about him were premature and naïve. Clearly Khrushchev believed in him, which was decisive backing for Zhivkov during this tumultuous period.

Zhivkov told me that his ideal for a true party leader was Khrushchev. He expressed delight in the speeches made by the Soviet leader, which confirmed my feeling that he deliberately copied Khrushchev's style. He even liked Khrushchev's eccentricity. Zhivkov's attitude, however, was totally subordinate: that of the victim who admires the one who bullies him.

Zhivkov proudly told me he had had two confrontations with the Soviet leader. I still remember his exact words: "Twice Khrushchev gave me a good hiding!" and added, "But I came out all right!" This word "hiding" expresses with great precision the nature of the relationship between the Soviet and Bulgarian leaderships, and shows the full subservience of Bulgarian leaders to their Soviet counterparts.

The whole country was full of jokes about Todor Zhivkov: he was always depicted as a cunning, primitive man of limited intellect. My personal impression from this long trip was that he was better than these popular evaluations gave him credit for and he was, at least in my opinion, superior to any of the other party leaders.

But it is clear that Zhivkov had little in common with the intelligentsia. He had obviously read very few books: he expressed himself with an unpleasant mixture of simple language and pompous phrases. He lacked in aesthetic sensibility. Nevertheless, behind all this stood a powerful, natural intellect, with quick reactions and an excellent memory. What he lacked, in my opinion, was imagination. In exchange for that he had a well developed intuitive sense. He was like an actor who had accepted his part, learned it well and performed contentedly, without having any wish to meddle in the role of the director or of the author of the play.

My disappointment with Todor Zhivkov's behaviour started long before the Warsaw Pact countries entered Czechoslovakia in August 1968. This was but the final point when all the masks were dropped. That was the moment when I perceived that all of the General Secretary's actions – all his public behaviour – were a logical consequence of his role in the Soviet theatrical called the "People's Republic of Bulgaria".

As an actor, Zhivkov had a particular talent for self-parody. This was best expressed when he recounted his hunting stories which he himself could not refrain from frequently laughing at. While listening to these tales, I gradually began to understand the larger significance of hunting to the higher party aristocracy.

In his broadcasts, Markov focused pointedly on the abuses of privilege, as exemplified by the passion for hunting. The prerogative of bored barons and rich landlords before the appearance of the Communist movement, now it had become the privilege of those who maintained they had come to power to seek and promote the happiness of the "working people". However, Zhivkov and the clique around him talked about hunting expeditions at special game reserves where access to ordinary people was absolutely forbidden. They discussed hunting junkets taken with other "important" foreign dignitaries. These occasions were replete with all the prescribed trappings – even with musical accompaniment.

To hunt, it seems, was a badge of good taste, an honourable hobby among the upper party circles of Eastern Europe. Hunting visits were often exchanged and special hunting rifles were presented on different occasions. Todor Zhivkov, for example, had travelled to Mongolia to hunt.

It occurred to Markov that even King Ferdinand or King Boris had never been hunting in Mongolia. "I asked myself: Why does Zhivkov go hunting? – Lenin was a hunter, Stalin was a hunter, Khrushchev was a hunter, Brezhnev, Walter Ulbricht, Ceausescu, Tito, Fidel Castro, Kim Il Sung, Enver Hodzha, all were hunters. Maybe the hobby of hunting was part of Marxism?"

Even after his defection, Georgi Markov remained a celebrity at home because of his talks on Radio Free Europe. Every week he broadcast a Bulgarian version of the Crossman Diaries, about what life was really like at the top. In Bulgaria as in other closed societies, there are many so-called forbidden areas, mainly concerning how the country is run and about the life styles of the Communist leaders.

One of Markov's broadcasts was called "Life Behind the Theocracies", in which he referred to the little curtains on the side and back of every official black Mercedes. He presented a gossipy but devastating picture of the corruption of absolute power, and he exposed the high living, loose morals, nepotism, financial abuses and status seeking proclivities of those who held power. As depicted by Markov, Pontius Pilate was a babe-in-arms compared to such leaders.

Markov talked about what he called the looking-glass world of Bulgarian Communism: he likened it to an Ionesco play of a deaf mute going to audition for a singing contest. To survive, one had to learn to translate from Bulgarian to Bulgarian: Markov explained that these are two totally different languages using exactly the same words. For instance, when they call someone the most beloved leader of the people, it really means he is the most hated person in the country.

Who was the second person living in the body of Georgi Markov? Most of us hide a different person other than the one we present to the world. No one is clearly black or white, but in the case of Markov the Jekyll and Hyde complex was expecially strong.

As a first step in our extensive investigation of Markov's life in Bulgaria before he left for the West, we drew up a long list of friends and acquaintances – which included ex-girl friends – and then we started visiting them. This was ongoing whilst democratic changes were just beginning in Bulgaria and so most of them were either afraid to talk or told us only things we already knew from the official eulogies of the recently acclaimed hero of the anti-Communist revolution.

Our first success was the discovery of one of Markov's closest friends and confidants, HD, with whom we met for three hour-long discussions. He was the main hero in one of Markov's best sellers, *A Portrait of My Double*. He is high up in the Bulgarian hierarchy, a close friend to the former Bulgarian Prime Minister, and is now the director of a prestigious cultural organisation in Bulgaria. HD's first words to us were:

> *Markov was a loser! He played with imagination, but he always lost. For him life was a big game, a game in which he wanted to play, to be in. He was charming – a street-wise charm*

which always impressed women. He had great success with women, but his only aim was to conquer them and then go back to his wife and cry on her shoulder about what a scoundrel he had been. He never bragged about his conquests. I was his only sexual confidant because of the absurd relationship we had with the same woman. Her name was Lina and she was one of the most beautiful women in Sofia. We used to arrange our secret sexual meetings in the same Sofia apartment, a few hours apart, and then later we would tell each other how things had gone. This went on until she found out, faced us with the truth, and we retorted by playing for her at cards. Georgi won. It was his only victory against me.

HD himself has had an unusual and chequered life. Born a few years after Markov, he graduated from Sofia University with a degree in English and French and was admitted immediately to the Foreign Office because of his high qualifications. Just as suddenly he was sacked because his father had had a small business before the revolution – a serious blow as his whole family was living on the small salary he received from his job at the Foreign Office.

Then, by chance, HD discovered he had a natural aptitude for card games, expecially poker. After losing his job, he continued to leave for work – or so his parents thought – but met instead with artists, writers, politicians and policemen to gamble for high stakes. (Poker was against the law, as was all gambling, except for the privileged.) He was a master, a true professional – a winner. At these games HD encountered another professional gambler, someone who lacked his own flair but who also invariably won from people who were born to lose. He was known as the "Hyena".

Markov also took part in these games and after the episode with the beautiful Lina, the three men became friends. Markov, however, was offended by the Hyena's success at the expense of weak opponents and so suggested to HD that they sting the Hyena. *A Portrait of My Double,* Markov's most acclaimed novel, describes the episode and comes the closest to revealing his private inner self.

Based on a real game with real people, the novel describes a poker game in which Markov is the star player. He makes a deal with "the man on his right" to rip off another player – the Hyena – by using a prearranged combination of stacked cards. But Markov loses because "the man on his right" has also made a deal with the Hyena. He deceives them both and is the only one who wins the jackpot.

HD was the archetype for "the man on his right". He narrates the episode in this way:

> I met Jerry (as I called Georgi Markov) through a friend who was an expert bridge and poker player. At the time, I was going through a difficult patch in my life. I had just been thrown out of the Foreign Office because my parents had had a private business before the Communist revolution in Bulgaria (in the early 50's).
>
> My friend offered me the possibility of earning money by playing poker for high stakes at gatherings where well known journalists, writers and intellectuals came to gamble away their money. (Under the Socialist system, these were the people who had money, and not businessmen as in the West.) They were referred to as "clients". There were two types of players: professionals and clients. I was a professional while Markov was a client. Quite naturally, we became friends – even more than friends since for a while we had a common lover, a girl called Lina who was one of the most beautiful women in Sofia.
>
> Another member of the group was a very aggressive player who did not know when to stop. His motto was "I want to see blood." In day-to-day life he had a good job and was more or less a nice person. We called him the Hyena.
>
> Markov had lost a lot of money to the Hyena and dreamed of "cleaning him up". I decided to help him, but I knew that the success of such an operation would depend on a lot of preparation. The Hyena, a very careful player, was well aware that money comes not from "hits" but from "turn over" (taking lots of small wins rather than playing for the jackpot).
>
> It took us two weeks to plan the whole operation. We bought identical decks of cards (in Bulgaria, poker is played with 32

Dissident or Professional Player?

cards) and examined them through a magnifying glass for production faults, and reproduced the ones we found. When the time for the game came, Jerry would have to be on my left side – that is why I am known as "the man on the right" – because he had to cut the cards in order for our sting to work. My role, however, was considerably more complicated: I had to substitute the cards with the ones which had previously been stacked. Not an easy task! In order to carry this off, I prepared for an entire week, practicing every day for two hours in front of a mirror.

Then came the night in question. Though it was a high stakes game, the atmosphere was calm. The Hyena always marked cards – the sevens and the eights – so at some point in the game I had to go to the kitchen to work the second deck of cards the same way. After three hours of play the moment we had been waiting for came. I made the change without a hitch – the cards had been in my pocket, as warm as if they had been in play.

The game continued and the cards were dealt. The pot was getting bigger. The Hyena had four kings to an an ace and was playing his usual aggressive game when there was an unexpected twist. The fourth player, Genadiev, suddenly said: "Three times the pot." I don't know what cards he held – maybe two pairs – but if things had gone wrong at this point, the cards Jerry was to receive might have gone to another player, and that would have spelled our undoing. But Markov made the best possible move in the situation; he said: "Nine times the pot." Though the Hyena thought for a long time, he was "in". Genadiev was, thank God, "out". After considering whether or not to discard the ace, the Hyena said: "Servi" ("No cards").

Jerry got his "kent flush" to the Jack of Clubs. The ensuing bidding was hot, but some sixth sense told the Hyena to stop in time. Nevertheless, he lost a lot of money. Markov won a lot but that was not important to him. Winning the "Big Hit" was all that mattered. The game was greater than him.

Years later, I gave a ride to a man who was hitchhiking. I took him to Sofia. Afterwards, my wife asked me if I knew the person. I replied: "That was the Hyena."

According to HD, the sting cost the Hyena a lot of money. Markov was absolutely exultant and said he had never felt happier in his whole life. Later, he told HD that he would never play poker again, as he could never hope to achieve another scoop like the one they had enacted.

That ended their poker partnership but started another based on a favourite maxim of Markov's which he had even written in one of his books: "The game is greater than life".

As HD told it: "In one of our philosophic discussions he started talking about another game – a game older than any other one. The game of power, played by the few who represent a club of initiated people. No matter who was politically at the top, this club was ongoing and always continued to pull the strings. He told me I could solve my problems and stop playing games for small stakes if I would join."

"And so, on Markov's recommendation and for many personal reasons, I joined the Bulgarian Secret Services or KDS. Two recommendations and extensive background research were needed – clearly my father's private business was not held against me this time; the second recommendation was arranged by Georgi Markov."

HD's subsequent career was quite successful. He was sent to Lebanon and to several Middle East countries where he dealt in arms and other not very respectable transactions. About ten years ago he retired from the active cloak and dagger business to become a respectable Bulgarian representative, businessman and manager. He ended our meeting with his own version of Markov's words: "If you are not a professional in a game, the game can kill you."

Several people who were close to Georgi Markov have told us of his connection with the Bulgarian Secret Service, the KDS. This relationship probably started through Yordan Ormankov with whom Markov became friendly during a long stay at a sanatorium, at the end of the Fifties.

Ormankov was then already a promising officer in the KDS. Later he became a colonel and a spokesman for the organisation. He retired a short time ago, but we talked to him on three different occasions. He has always maintained that he and Markov were good friends, but refused to comment on any involvement on Markov's part in intelligence work. But then, Ormankov is a professional – a member of the "Club" – who considers that files and intelligence personnel should remain secret and confidential, independent of the political changes that bring new masters to power.

Nina Vejinova, the widow of Pavel Vejinov (one of Bulgaria's most highly regarded writers; he died a few years ago), told us that her husband had warned her never to say anything in front of Markov which she would not want the KDS to hear. At the time, she was rather startled because Vejinov and Markov were supposed to be good friends and often played high stakes poker together. Nina Vejinova is alive and active in Bulgaria. She was one of the few people to openly praise our book when it was first published. Though most of the people who knew Markov agreed in private with our assessment of his character, they were not willing to go on the record.

At the time of the first edition of this book, we were certain that Georgi Markov had at the least been an informer for the KDS, a view based on various lines of evidence. For the TV serial *We Are at Every Kilometre* Markov was allowed access to the archives of the Bulgarian Communist Party. These archives were one of the most guarded secrets of the Bulgarian State and only members of the all powerful Politburo and high ranking KDS officials had access to them. How else, therefore, could Markov have looked through them at will?

Also, Markov owned the first BMW car in Bulgaria. Such a car could be obtained only through UBO – one of the branches of the Security Services. He obtained a passport valid for six months and good for travel to all countries of the world, a privilege normally reserved only for someone very high up and close in the hierarchy to a "Chenge" (a slang word in Bulgarian meaning a secret policeman).

The evidence strongly suggests that the other Georgi Markov was a man who had learned by surviving how to play the "big game" of espionage.

Chapter IV
The Game in Other Places

Events which happened after the publication of this book in Bulgaria not only substantiated our theories but showed that things were even more serious than we had at first thought. The problems encountered by the Bulgarian investigators were emblematic of the larger Soviet system which dominated them, and have far reaching consequences which painfully touch the lives of innocent people, even in the "free" West.

Just when it looked as though the Bulgarian investigation was thoroughly bogged down by conjectures, questions without answers and newspaper gossip, the Soviet Bloc started to crumble and astounding revelations began to slip through the usual net of secrecy and intimidation. The defection of high ranking KGB officials together with disclosures from on high both furthered and signalled this process of political disintegration.

In 1985, Oleg Gordievsky, who at that time was the chief of the KGB's London station, defected. Subsequently, he collaborated with Christopher Andrew (a noted Cambridge historian) in writing *KGB: An Inside Story*. Their book (published in London in 1990 – see Reference section, page 99) is a history of the KGB's foreign operations from Lenin to Gorbachev. One of the more sensational assertions in the book claimed to identify the fifth "mole" in the British Secret Service as John Cairncross. (The other Soviet agents had long been identified as Philby, Burgess, Maclean and Blunt.)

Attention became focused on Cairncross's denial of this allegation which, unfortunately, detracted from other and more significant facts brought to light by Andrew and Gordievsky. Neither of the authors believed in the conspiracy theory which held that Western intelligence services and international Zionism were plotting in concert to cause the downfall of the Soviet Union. They asserted, however, that the KGB had always believed this to be the case and feared the possible consequences. This scare heavily influenced decisions made in KGB circles during the "Prague Spring" of 1968, events which the KGB considered to be the personal betrayal of Dubcek (previously known to the KGB as "our Sasha").

As a result of this, says Gordievsky, the Czechoslovak Interior Ministry had to report, on orders from Moscow, on all employees of Jewish origin. Another sign of the KGB's paranoia was the breaking of an old internal rule which prohibits spying within "People's Republics" and, therefore, homes of reformers were bugged and KGB "defectors to the West" were sent to Prague as tourists, to monitor the activities of suspected dissidents.

The picture in Poland in 1981 was very similar. KGB "defectors to the West", who were working for the KGB, were sent to Warsaw and Gdansk to find out if "Solidarity" was as popular as the KGB considered it to be. According to Gordievsky, Moscow maintained that the best "Solidarity" activists were Jews.

Another fact disclosed in Andrew and Gordievsky's book concerns Moscow's reluctance to undertake military intervention in Poland. At the time, most experts in the West considered that Moscow was ready for action. The KGB, for its part, was convinced that the western secret services had collaborated with "Solidarity" to create undercover structures and groups for guerrilla warfare in Poland. Thus, the only solution for the KGB was a military coup organised by the Polish army with General Jaruzelski assuming the presidency. According to Gordievsky, Jaruzelski had agreed to this plan and the KGB considered him as "their man in Warsaw." The only hitch was that Brezhnev, who was old and ill, had to be asked twice before he gave his consent to the plan.

The same fear of conspiracy led the KGB's Washington Chief of Station to suspect that there was a plot by opponents of

1. Markov (left) as a boy with his mother and brother, Nikola

2. Markov (left) and his first wife Zdravka (far right), witnessing the marriage of friends

3. Markov (left) with Ormankov at a TB sanatorium at Bladaya

4. Markov (far left) and other writers and intellectuals with Zhivkov (second from right), on a hunting expedition

5. Markov in Bulgaria

6. The wedding with Annabelle

7. Markov (right) with his brother Nikola and wife Annabelle in England 1975

8. Markov and Nikola in England

9. Markov with Annabelle and daughter Sasha

10. Markov with Sasha

11. Dr David Gall, head of toxicology lab at Porton Down

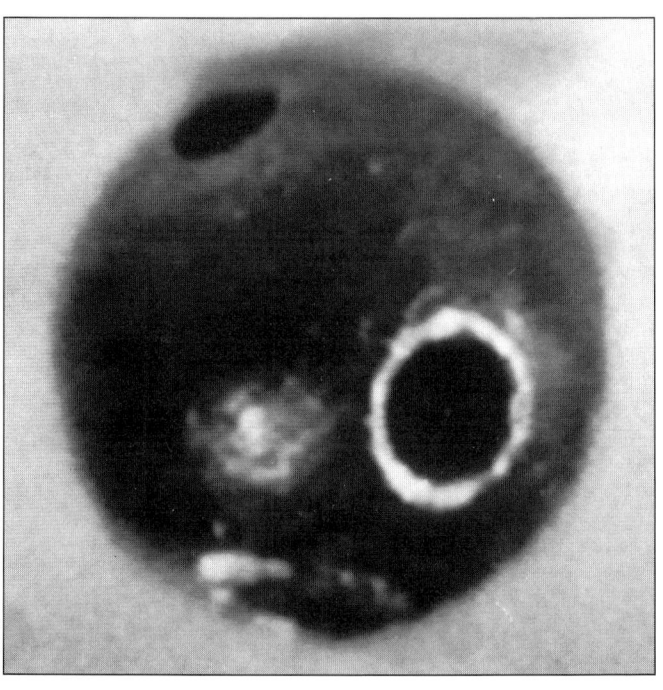

12. The ricin pellet that was removed from Markov's thigh

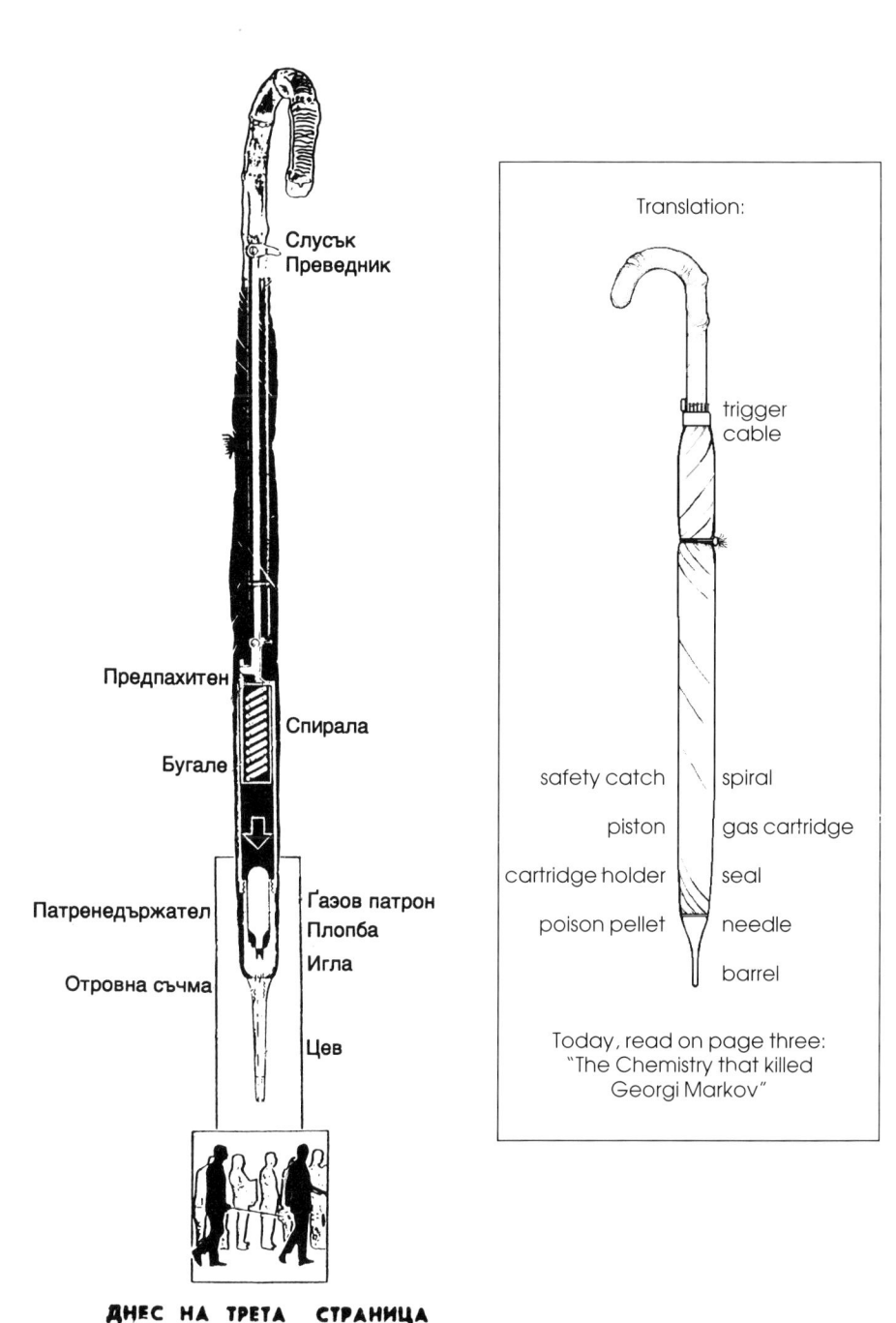

13. Fanciful cross-section of the "poison umbrella gun" from a Bulgarian newspaper

14. (top) Vladimir Kostov, Bulgarian journalist and émigré
15. (bottom) Oleg Kalugin, former Major-General of the KGB

16. (top) Kyril Panov, head of the Bulgarian Section of Radio Free Europe
17. (bottom left) Dimitar Stoyanov, former Bulgarian Minister for Internal Affairs
18. (bottom right) Vlado Todorov, high ranking officer in the Bulgarian KDS

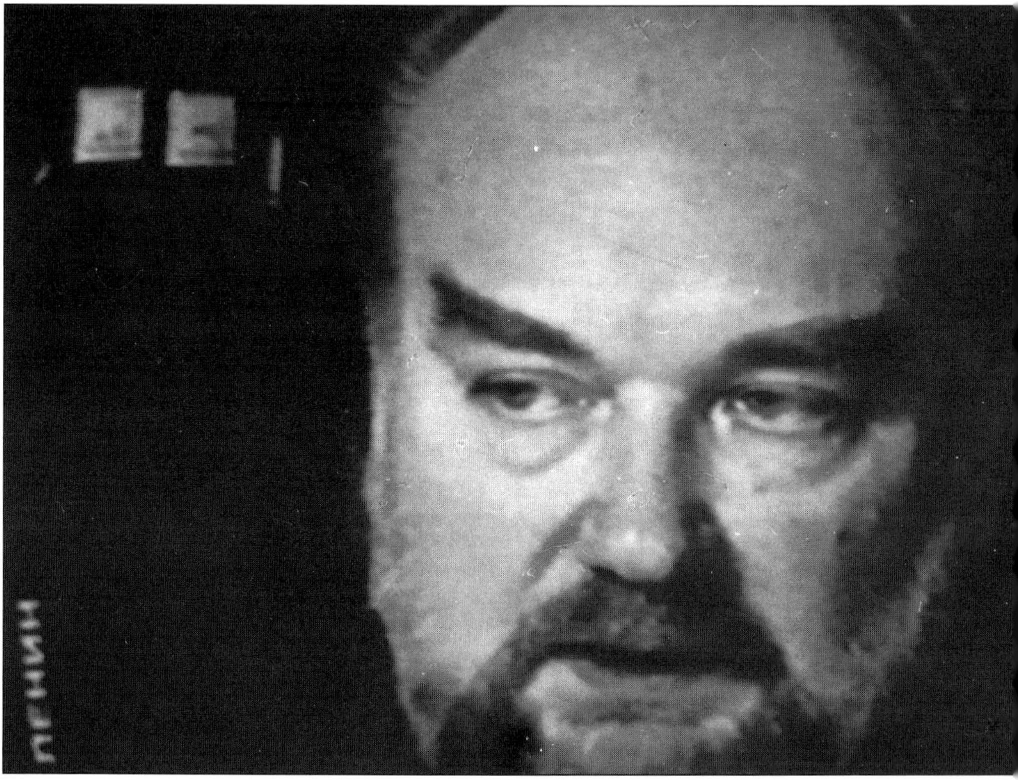
ЛЕНИН

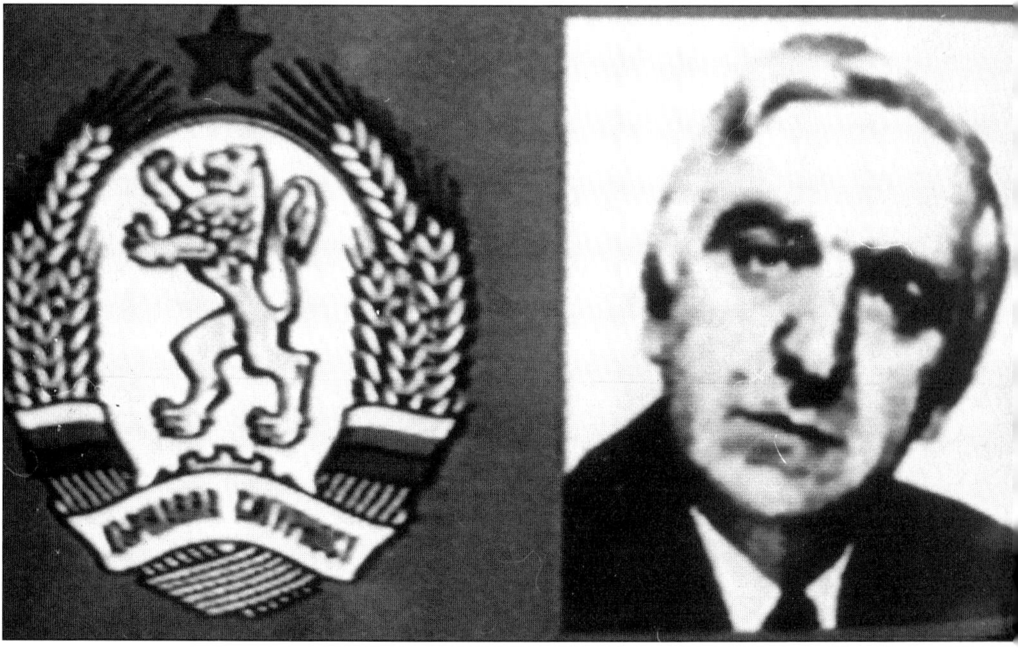

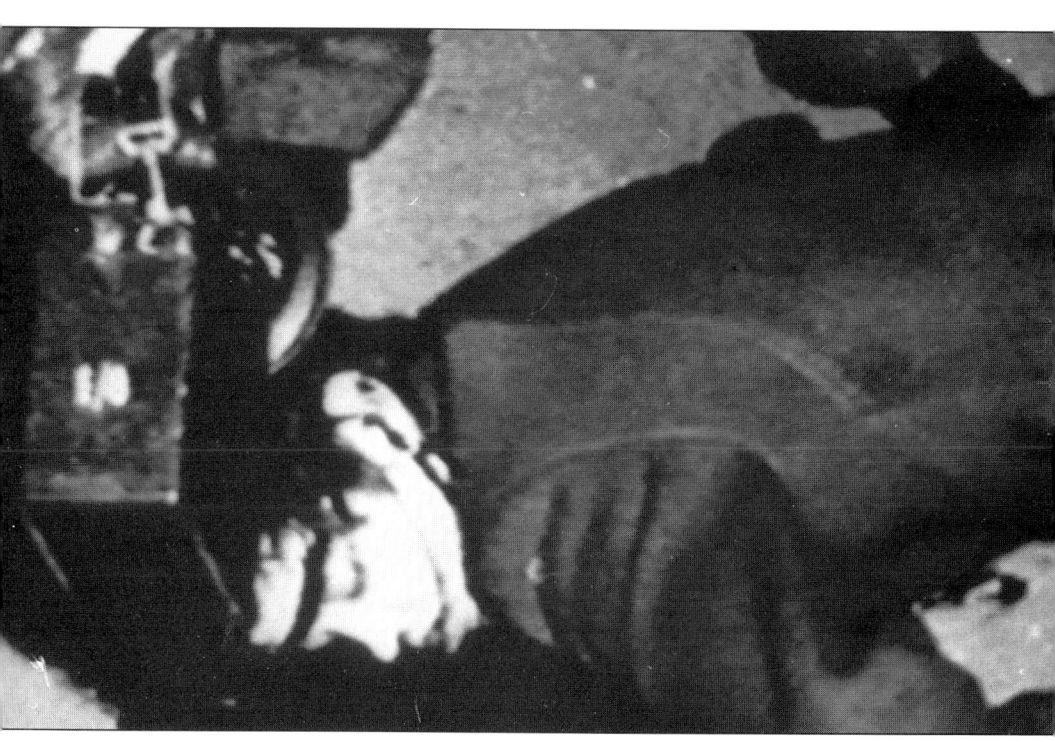

21. Police photograph of the body of Vassilena Stolyova, one of a group murdered in Vienna

19. (opposite top) Nikolai Khokhlov, KGB officer who specialised in political murder
20. (opposite bottom) Boris Arsov, Bulgarian immigrant murdered a short time before Markov

22. Jelyo Jelev, President of Bulgaria, putting flowers on Markov's grave in Dorset

improved relations with the Soviet Union, especially Zionists, to topple the US president, Richard Nixon.

According to Andrew and Gordievsky's book, the KGB's main weakness was its lack of understanding of the Western world and its attitudes. This lack of understanding had already brought the world close to a nuclear holocaust. Moreover, because the KGB was convinced that the West was preparing a nuclear first strike against the USSR, they had placed agents all over the Western world to be on the lookout for signs of an imminent attack. These agents were ordered to compile detailed observations on a wide spectrum of aspects of everyday life in the West. For example, they were to count how many windows had lights on after hours in government buidings, to monitor blood prices at blood banks in Great Britain, and to observe the activities of churches and major financial institutions.

KGB agents were encouraged to utilise any source of information in order to detect the least sign of a coming attack. Were no such evidence apparent, they fabricated it. If the KGB Centre suspected falsifications, it did not consider the invention of facts as sufficient reason to doubt the existence of the consipiracy.

Andrew and Gordievsky's book vividly reveals the extent of the Soviet xenophobia which engendered the expansion of KGB activities, including the Markov case. Out of the 704 pages of the book, only one and a half deal specifically with the Markov murder, in which the authors incorrectly favour the umbrella theory.

Furthermore, they claim that the umbrella was designed in the KGB's technical laboratory not as a shooting device, but as a syringe-topped weapon which injects poison. To kill with such a weapon would require the skill of a surgeon and, in addition, would entail no mean feat of swordsmanship. The blow from the sword umbrella would have to be light enough not to alarm the victim and yet deep enough to successfully inject the poison.

Scotland Yard, however, never believed in the umbrella theory. They believed the murderer used the picking up of the fallen umbrella to mask his shot with an air pistol. From his bent over position he would have had an ideal view of Markov's upper thigh. In June 1991, Scotland Yard detectives and Bulgarian investigators made a joint statement in Sofia disclaiming the umbrella theory. Our book, which had been published in the Bulgarian press in the summer of 1990, also rejected the umbrella theory.

At the end of March 1991, the Kalugin disclosures first resounded through the whole world's media. Oleg Danailovich Kalugin, a major-general of the KGB, was suddenly retired at the age of 55, in February 1990. He was given the meagre pension of 350 roubles a month (about $18 US) and a bonus of 7000 roubles for excellent service. This was certainly not the note on which we would expect one of the most successful careers in the KGB since World War II to end.

Kalugin was less than 40 when he was appointed chief of the department for external counter intelligence after lengthy and clearly very successful missions in some Western countries. Seven years later he was moved to Leningrad (now St Petersburg) as deputy chief of the Leningrad KGB. From 1987 until his untimely retirement he was back in Moscow at KGB headquarters in Dzerzhinsky Square. Throughout his career he was in competition with his notorious colleague, Vladimir Kryuchkov, who became head of the KGB and will now stand trial for treason after the unsuccessful coup in the Soviet Union in 1991.

Why did the KGB get rid of one of their most experienced executives who had been awarded 22 state medals? There are two probable reasons. The first was Kalugin's activity in Leningrad, where he masterminded the investigation for corruption against 40 high up party officials. When clues started leading to the Kremlin, the investigation was stopped and Kalugin was sent back to Moscow.

The second reason was the personal animosity that had been growing between Kalugin and Kryuchkov. A few months after his retirement, the major-general, in a reserved but enthusiastic defence of Socialism, provoked his ex-colleagues and bosses and the whole "Lublyanka". At the 16th June 1990 conference of the group "Democratic Platform" inside the Soviet Communist Party, Kalugin talked about his work in the KGB and gave an astounding analysis of the methods used by the Soviet Secret Service.

A few days later he gave interviews to the newspapers *Moscow News* and *Komsomolskaya Pravda* and to Soviet television. His disclosures were shocking not because of their content (which was already well known by every senior school student in the Soviet Union), but because these comments appeared openly in the mass media.

The substance of Kalugin's allegations was that the KGB had recruited and infiltrated their agents into all spheres of Soviet society, from members of the Academy of Sciences to the Police, musicians and literary critics. The KGB bugged telephones and opened correspondence, and files were kept on an astounding number of ordinary citizens. Agents routinely broke into people's flats, and distributed disinformation and malicious gossip. KGB laboratories used lethal substances and weapons that endangered the life and health of the population.

Kalugin further asserted that many of the officials in the KGB leaned to the "right" and that, instead of defending the security of the country and its citizens, it had become the main support of the reactionary, authoritarian forces. Kalugin made an unprecedented appeal for the de-politicisation of the KGB, for its subordination to Parliament and to the Soviet legislature, for the full reorganisation of the KGB, for the sacking of fifty per cent of its personnel, and for a stop to the use of paid informers and all surveillance on political grounds.

The leadership of the KGB reacted instantly. The answer came on the pages of *Pravda* on the 28th of June 1990, and it was written in the style and with the methods of the "iron crusaders of the revolution" from the not so distant past. Kalugin was accused of professional incompetence bordering on treason and with trumped up charges of drunkenness and sexual orgies, which he had supposedly indulged in through the use of his official position and to satisfy his revengeful nature.

On June 30th, Gorbachev issued a decree which revoked all of Kalugin's state medals, while the Council of Ministers took away his pension and rank of general. The State Prosecutor's Office started an investigation against Kalugin for divulging state secrets.

However, having just won the parliamentary election in Krasnodar (which gave him parliamentary immunity), Kalugin was not to be intimidated. On the pages of *The International Herald Tribune* he went on to accuse the KGB of full knowledge of the help, training and support given by the East German Secret Police to terrorist groups such as the "Red Brigades" and the "Baader-Meinhoff Gang", which had continued their activities as late as 1990. Kalugin confirmed that the most notorious terrorist, known by the name of Carlos, had come and gone many times from East Berlin during the seventies. Kalugin said: "We kept an eye on him, so we would know what he was planning. Naturally, publicly, we said we had never heard of him."

At this point it is important to question whether Kalugin was truly seeking to tell all about the KGB, or if he was simply acting as a politician – which he had only recently become – and was, therefore, also playing for high stakes.

To begin with, all the facts he disclosed about the KGB were well known to the Western press. Although the fact that he was saying these things rocked the façade of the KGB, his disclosures did not significantly budge the main structure. Kalugin was, is and will always be a member of the "Club": he would never go against the cardinal prohibition by giving away real secrets. He probably knew about the possibility of the coming coup attempt and gambled on its failure. As an excellent intelligence officer, he assessed the situation correctly and won, with his rank behind him and a bright political future in front of him. However, in one of his interviews after the coup, Kalugin clearly stated that he did not think the KGB was on the agenda or that it would be right to dismantle the secret services network.

The first time Kalugin talked about Georgi Markov was during an interview for Radio Liberty. He stated that in 1978 Vladimir Kryuchkov (who was then chief of the KGB intelligence department) and his Deputy General Usatov, had invited him (Kalugin) to accompany them to Yuri Andropov's office. Andropov was then Chief of the KGB and later became General Secretary of the Central Committee of the Soviet Communist Party.

Kryuchkov reported to Andropov that a letter or telegram (Kalugin does not remember precisely) had been received from the Bulgarian Minister for Internal Affairs, Dimitar Stoyanov. The message contained a request for help in the physical destruction of the dissident writer Georgi Markov who, through the privilege of past closeness to the family of Todor Zhivkov (the Communist leader of Bulgaria), knew many facts about Zhivkov's private life. After defecting to the West, Markov started working at the BBC and Radio Free Europe, broadcasting programmes against Communism and against Zhivkov personally.

Hearing this, Andropov started to pace his office silently and after awhile said: "I am against political murders. It does not matter who is asking us for such services, we should keep clear of such actions."

At that moment (according to Kalugin), Kryuchkov reminded Andropov that this was a personal request from the Bulgarian President and General Secretary of the Communist Party. If refused, Zhivkov might form the impression that the attitude of the Soviet leadership towards Bulgaria was not as warm as was publicly and officially stated.

After some thought, Andropov said: "All right, but there must be no personal Soviet involvement! Send them specialists, send them the necessary equipment and special devices, show them how to use everything and that is it! I am against any other form of participation. That is all!"

Following this meeting in Andropov's office and in keeping with the discussion and decisions reached, Kalugin, as Chief of External Counter-Intelligence, sent two of his men to Sofia. They were Sergei Michaylovich Golubev (chief of the security section of the Intelligence Department of the KGB) and a specialist in untraceable poisons (whose identity it has been impossible to determine). On arrival in the Bulgarian capital, the two were received by the then chief of Bulgarian Intelligence, Vasil Kotsev, and the two Russians began training the Bulgarian colleagues who had been entrusted with the execution of Markov.

Kalugin had a long discussion with Golubev after his return from Sofia. The first plan to "neutralise" Markov consisted of applying a special poisonous cream to his skin. They knew he was soon going on vacation somewhere in the Mediterranean area, so the cream was to be applied to his skin while he was on the beach among the crowds of sunbathers. Only a small dab of the cream would be needed to stop the heart during the next 24 hours. According to Kalugin, this cream is a standard lethal weapon in the KGB arsenal. For reasons which neither Golubev nor Kalugin could explain, this plan was aborted.

The second plan called for the same poison to be used orally in a drink during lunch or dinner. Kalugin maintains that this plan was put into action somewhere close to Munich, but that Markov survived without even suspecting that an attempt had been made on his life. That is when the London phase of the criminal experiment was given the green light. It was decided that the victim would be shot with a lethal pellet filled with the same poison. The shot would be made with a special contraption that looks and functions like an umbrella, but which is in fact an air pistol.

In his interview for Radio Liberty, Kalugin was very specific on this point, saying that the shooting umbrella was designed and constructed in the KGB Laboratory 13, a laboratory created under Stalin and Beria. The chief of the laboratory during the period mentioned by Kalugin was Viktor Chebrikov, one of the KGB bosses who later became a Politburo member and secretary of the Central Committee of the Soviet Communist Party.

The three murder instruments – the poison, the pellet and the umbrella – had to be tested after their arrival in Sofia. Then (according to Kalugin), in a test situation, an agent of the Bulgarian KDS shot a man sentenced to death with the murder kit from a distance of about three feet. In spite of the lethalness of the poison, the intended victim remained alive. Golubev immediately returned to Moscow for additional consultations after which, and in spite of the set-back, the plan was adopted. The murder was to have been carried out on a beach in Italy where Markov was on holiday, but for some reason this plan also failed. Not to be deterred, the plan was finally carried out on Waterloo Bridge in London. Then (according to Kalugin in the interview for Radio Liberty), the murderer, encouraged by his success, shot Vladimir Kostov, three days later in Paris.

Five months had passed since the first meeting in Andropov's office.

The greatest Kalugin fiasco occurred at the press conference he held in Sofia in September 1992. Invited by the Bulgarian President, Jelyo Jelev, Kalugin was asked to visit Bulgaria and give evidence to the investigators of the Markov murder as a witness in the case.

At the end of Kalugin's three-day stay in Bulgaria, a press conference was organised for him in the Palace of Culture. He was accompanied by Rumen Danov, the security advisor to President Jelev. The press conference started with a statement by Kalugin in which he repeated his Radio Liberty story but with certain omissions and changes. In this version, the umbrella was used as cover for the air pistol shot at Markov, and there was no mention either of the attempt on Vladimir Kostov's life or of Laboratory 13 of the KGB.

Traditionally at big press conferences, TV reporters get the first chance to put questions. Vladimir Bereanu was then anchoring a popular late night news show on Bulgarian TV and so was the first to question Kalugin. The whole press conference, picture and sound, has been recorded on video tape in the archives of Bulgarian National Television. The following is from that press conference:

B: Mr Kalugin, as one of the bosses of the all-powerful KGB, you are supposed to have excellent memory and great capability to analyse facts. How come you have made so many mistakes and have corrected your story so many times? I refer to the poisonous umbrella which in your first story was constructed more or less under your supervision in Laboratory 13 and then, after the truth about the umbrella was reported to you, it suddenly vanished into thin air, and to the incorrect dates and sequence of events in the murder of Markov and the attempted murder of Kostov.

K: *It might seem strange to you, but our memories also fail. Anyway, how the murder was done and the exact dates are not important. The important fact is that we helped our colleagues from the KDS to kill Markov on the orders of Todor Zhivkov, who hated the writer for his broadcasts on Radio Free Europe. That is what is important.*

B: *But in your original story the murder was done with a poison tipped umbrella and the attempt on Kostov was made three days after the Markov murder. This is exactly what Gordievsky says in his book which was published long before your confessions. Maybe you are just repeating Gordievsky's errors? You have probably read your colleague's book?*

K: *No, I have not read his book. These errors, as you call them, are just coincidences.*

B: *But Mr Kalugin, if your story is true and the correct facts are that the attempt on Kostov's life was made ten days before the Markov murder, what was the reason for the attempt on Kostov? He never wrote or said anything against Zhivkov.*

K: *I don't know. All I can do is guess that the KDS tried out the poison on Kostov before murdering Markov. Kostov was a traitor anyway.*

B: *But that has no logic.*

K: *Why?*

B: *Because although the attempt on Kostov failed, they went on to use the same method on the intended victim.*

At this point, all the journalists present started to laugh.

K: I am here to give evidence. Not to be harrassed about unimportant details.

Until this, Kalugin was in an earnest open mood, but the last remark was made with impatience and a steely look in his eyes. Suddenly he was facing about sixty unbelieving journalists. The rest of the press conference went badly for him and ended on an ominous note. The last question was put by a young woman from the newspaper *Trud*.

Trud: Mr Kalugin, why are you here and not in prison?

K: What do you mean?

Trud: Well, if what you say is true, then you are clearly guilty of conspiracy to commit murder. You should be arrested.

K: I'm here to give evidence. I am ready to face a trial and the consequences of my action, but I don't think it will come to that.

This is where Mr Danov, who had by this time become restless, ended the press conference, twenty minutes earlier than was planned, pleading fatigue on Kalugin's part.

Kalugin went on to other countries telling new and breathtaking stories about the KGB in that Dr Strangelovian manner of his. One of his most recent stories was published in *The Sunday Times* on the 12th of September 1993. According to his latest "media bomb", Soviet generals considered building a "seismic bomb" that could be exploded underground to devastate America with earthquakes and tidal waves. No comment is needed on this except to say that the original idea for it had been published in the early 20's in the novel, *The Ruler of the World* by the Russian science fiction author, Alexander Belyaev. So "Club" member Oleg Kalugin goes on telling bedtime stories and, if believed, he is above the law because he has still not been held accountable for his part in the murder of Georgi Markov.

Kalugin's interview caused an enormous outcry in Bulgaria. Public awareness had already been alerted by the publication of our book. Bereanu, a newscaster and presenter of the late night news show on Channel One of Bulgarian Television, commented in the course of the show on the Kalugin revelations. He pointed out three very important inconsistencies in Kalugin's version of what had happened.

First, the umbrella was not used as the weapon and was not, therefore, directly involved in the killing, casting doubt on the claim by Kalugin of the involvement of Laboratory 13.

Second, according to Kostov's wife, her husband was shot ten days before Markov, not three days after.

Third, if the murder of Markov had been ordered by Zhivkov for the reasons given by Kalugin, why had the murderer then tried to kill Kostov as well? Was he a homicidal maniac, or was he perhaps in love with Kostov's wife, or maybe he hoped to receive a bonus for killing another "enemy of the people"?

There were two other minor inconsistencies. First, the poison ricin cannot be used in any cream: its lethal effect would be neutralised by contact with the moisture of another substance. Second, according to Kalugin's version, there were about 14 people involved in the planning of this murder, making it one of the most unprofessional murders in the long history of killing either for the KGB or the KDS.

Following the author's televised comments, Asen Geshakov (the Moscow correspondent of Bulgarian TV) managed to get an exclusive interview with Kalugin, which was subsequently shown on Bulgarian TV. When Geshakov pressed him on all the points presented above, Kalugin – without batting an eyelid – changed his story. In his revised account there was no umbrella air gun; an umbrella had been used only as cover for the shot which was made with a pistol.

As far as the mistake about when the Kostov shooting took place, Kalugin claimed that his memory had slipped. He disclaimed any knowledge of why the Bulgarians had shot Kostov but suggested that perhaps they were trying out their method before using it on Markov.

If that were so, and given that the experiment had in fact failed, why did they go on to shoot Markov?

Suddenly the super spy – the intelligence expert, the man whose main job and skill had been to gather facts and analyse them – *appeared* to be muddled and suffering from memory lapses. This seemed rather implausible.

When Geshakov asked why Kalugin was only then revealing all these facts on the Markov murder, rather than when he had been "retired" from the KGB, Kalugin replied that he was now ready to speak out because of the trial against Todor Zhivkov.

Chapter V
A Wilderness of Mirrors

The palace coup in Sofia (10th of November 1989) removed the Communist dictator of 36 years, Todor Zhivkov. Not long after, a series of unconvincing statements were made. First, accused of petty financial fraud and unlawful income, Zhivkov's ex-cronies started a trial against him. How ironic that the man under whom hundreds of people had been killed or imprisoned, and who had destroyed the Bulgarian economy, was being charged with stealing a few trifling quid!

Later, having also been accused of ordering Markov's murder, Zhivkov gave an interview to *The Times* in which he categorically denied having had any involvement in it. We talked to him on three different occasions. During one of these talks he suggested that the murder might have been committed by the Bulgarian Secret Services without his knowledge, but this would have been most unlikely.

Kalugin maintained all along that Zhivkov was the organiser of the Markov murder and he was ready to testify to this at a trial against Zhivkov in Sofia. As evidence in support of his allegations, Kalugin showed us a Belgian Browning hand gun with a personal inscription which says: "From the Bulgarian Minister of the Interior, Dimitar Stoyanov, to Oleg Kalugin." Although the inscription does not say for what services the present had been awarded, Kalugin maintained that it was for his help in arranging the murder of Markov.

The ex-Minister for Home Affairs (in Bulgaria, called Minister of the Interior), Dimitar Stoyanov now lives in a luxury flat in one of the best parts of Sofia. We spent a week trying to talk to him, but he had gone underground. Finally, we managed to contact him by phone. According to him, everything Kalugin had said was slander. "I never made any requests to Andropov or Kryuchkov for help in removing Georgi Markov."

We might have discounted this as another unprovable disclaimer but for a strange mistake which Stoyanov made during our conversations: he said Kalugin was an ex-KGB officer who had gone over to the British in 1984. Had Stoyanov confused Kalugin with Gordievsky? If so, why had Kalugin said he knew Stoyanov personally?

The inconsistencies, sudden changes, and the general inaccuracies of Kalugin's story make it difficult to accept his credibility. However, according to our investigations, one part of it is true: that the KDS and Stoyanov had asked the KGB for help in the elimination of Georgi Markov and Vladimir Kostov. Andropov probably did react as represented by Kalugin, and Kryuchkov did explain why such action was necessary.

The explanation for why he did so, however, is completely different. The motive for the murder is the key to the whole mystery.

According to Kalugin's version of the story, Todor Zhivkov hated Markov because of his broadcasts and so ordered the murder; Stoyanov went to the KGB for help; the KGB grudgingly acquiesced; and, after a series of blunders, an agent (Woodpecker) killed Markov, and that was that. Zhivkov was the culprit; and everyone else was just following orders – like in Nazi Germany.

But is this really credible? Were those broadcasts, presented earlier, enough to infuriate Zhivkov to the point of ordering the murder of Markov? We do not think so. Mr Oleg Kalugin (once more a general) was trying to shift the blame for Markov's murder to Zhivkov, in order to remove the same blame from the KGB, the KDS and from himself.

The man who for thirty years had worked for one of the most fearsome and horrible organisations, the KGB, the man who according to his own statements had sent two specialists to Sofia to prepare the murders of Markov and Kostov, the man who took the decision together with Andropov and Kryuchkov to help the Bulgarians in their "heroic" action, would now have us believe that he is a born democrat, a fighter for the truth – a crusader.

While all this was going on, Stanko Todorov (for many years a member of the Bulgarian Politburo of the Central Committee of the Bulgarian Communist Party, twice Prime Minister of Bulgaria during the time of Markov's murder, and twice Chairman of the Bulgarian Parliament) agreed to talk to us concerning the Markov case.

Going to meet him took us to one of the best neighbourhoods of Sofia, where many of the people who normally could only be glimpsed behind the curtains of official Mercedes cars, or on portraits in offices, or at the rostrum of big government conferences, lived and still live. These days there are no longer any bodyguards. We rang twice and the door opened promptly. The man himself – who for many years had represented the Party and the government leadership – greeted us.

The flat is furnished expensively and with taste but looks surprisingly small. There is marble in the hall and the walls are adorned with expensive paintings by Bulgarian painters. A big bookcase still holds the works of Marx, Engels and Lenin. Although he was still in good form, perhaps the recent failure of the old ideas had caused him to look old and a little haggard. We asked about Markov but the only thing we managed to get from him was a firm statement that the Politburo had never discussed Georgi Markov, and that no decision to "remove" Markov, as our host put it, had ever been taken.

This was either a blank wall or the truth.

The next step for us was to make a quick visit to Moscow, where one of us met the retired General Ivan Tichonovich Savchenko, the man who had been the KGB Chief of Station in Bulgaria at the time of Markov's murder. He told us categorically: "No discussions, and no direct or written requests were made by the Bulgarian side on the subject of Georgi Markov or of his elimination."

Savchenko had been an official representative of the KGB in Bulgaria from 1969 to 1980, in which capacity he had been present at all meetings between the Soviet and Bulgarian Security Services. All other contacts between the KGB and KDS were made through him, which is why he was certain that there had been no request made to Andropov from Dimitar Stoyanov for help in killing the famous Bulgarian émigré.

In Savchenko's words (taken directly from the cassette recording we made during the interview): "Had it been in written form, it would have had to go through me for encoding. I have never received such a request orally or in written form. I have been present at all discussions between the leadership of Soviet and Bulgarian intelligence and the murder of Georgi Markov has never been discussed."

Savchenko maintains that the murder was organised by one of the Western intelligence agencies: "I remember that when, in the autumn of 1978, the Western press made a big fuss over Markov's death, we had information that the British Secret Service was looking for clues leading to the KGB and the KDS, and after a thorough analysis of all facts we came to the conclusion that the murder had been done by one of the Western secret services with the aim of discrediting the Bulgarian regime and its security services. The general opinion was that the murder had been executed by the CIA, as it was in their style. I can declare that neither the Soviet nor the Bulgarian authorities had anything to do with the murder of Georgi Markov."

Another member of the "Club" – another blank wall.

Accelerating events proved the General wrong. During the spring meeting with Army General Semerdjiev, who was then Minister of the Interior and is now Bulgaria's Vice President, we asked the General if there was any file on Georgi Markov in the KDS (which had subsequently been removed). He answered negatively.

However, in June 1991, Dr Jelyo Jelev, the President of Bulgaria and the leading figure in the struggle against the totalitarian regime in the country, made a dramatic appearance on national television and announced that a file on Georgi Markov had existed in the archives of the KDS up to the beginning of 1990. According to Jelev, it had since been destroyed.

While the media had its day gossiping and speculating about whether or not there was a file on Markov and, if so, what it might or might not mean, we managed to uncover who had held the file and what had happened to this decisive document, which might hold the solution to the Markov mystery. By talking to General Semerdjiev (at that time Vice President) and to a few contacts in the new security services (who, not surprisingly, prefer to remain anonymous) we were subsequently able to reconstruct what had happened.

General Semerdjiev, in his capacity as the then Minister of the Interior, ordered his Deputy Minister Savov to bring him Markov's file. Savov, in turn, ordered General Vlado Todorov to get Markov's file from General Serkedjieva (she was chief of the archives of the Ministry of the Interior) and, after studying it carefully, to destroy it. In this scenario, General Vlado Todorov was the last person to hold Markov's file.

Vlado Todorov had graduated from the well known school of the Soviet KGB in Moscow and then served as Chief of State Security in the Bulgarian cities of Varna and Dobrich. Later he became deputy chief of intelligence responsible for Western Europe, the USA, Canada and Japan. He succeeded to the post previously held by General Vasil Kotsev (who, according to Kalugin, had received the two KGB lethal-weapons specialists, and who died in mysterious circumstances in 1986). It is an open secret that Todorov's promotion to this post had been forwarded by Vladilen Fyodorov, the ex-Chief of Station of the KGB in Bulgaria and Chief Counsellor to the Minister of the Interior,

Dimitar Stoyanov. The close friendship between Fyodorov and Todorov is intensified by the fact that Todorov's wife is Russian.

The moment we had this information we tried to get in touch with General Todorov, who now lives in a luxury block of flats close to the Soviet Embassy. We were not, however, the only ones looking for Todorov. The two state investigators trying to unravel the Markov mystery were also on his trail, but he seemed to have disappeared without a trace. Bulgarian newspapers investigating the whole web of intrigue surrounding Markov's murder concluded that he had gone to the Soviet Union. We managed to get his Moscow address and to seek him out there.

When we met General Todorov he explained that he had been in Moscow since the beginning of May 1991, due to a family situation. (His wife's mother had to move to a new house and he had come to help.) At the same time he wanted to have a complete health check, as he had not been feeling well for a year (coincidental with the fall of the totalitarian regime); he had had a nervous breakdown and had lost twenty pounds. Then, ten days after arriving in Moscow, Todorov had a heart attack. Since that time he had mostly stayed in bed and had gone out only rarely.

It was difficult to get Todorov to answer any questions at all, but finally he did respond to some:

Q *Why did you destroy Markov's file?*

A *The Ministry of the Interior periodically destroys old files and this one was in my possession, so . . .*

Q *Why was it in your possession?*

A *Because General Savov ordered me to see if "we had anything to do with Markov's murder" and then he ordered me to destroy it.*

Q *Do you think you are guilty of destroying important evidence?*

A *I accept all responsibility for my actions. My hands are clean.*

Q *Do you think of returning to Bulgaria?*

A *The doctors have ordered me to go to a sanatorium, but after all this commotion in Bulgaria I might go back sooner.*

Q What did Markov's file contain?

A Nothing important. Just information about his work for the BBC and Radio Free Europe. It was what we call a "personal" file.

Q What does that mean?

A The Ministry of the Interior kept two types of files. The first, called "personal" files, are started, filed and updated by the sixth department, the one which deals with political enemies and dissidents. The second are called "working" files and in those files we keep information about our agents and their activities, reports and so on . . .

That was the end of our first interview with Vlado Todorov. At the time we thought that it would be the last, but events were to prove us wrong.

During this same trip to Moscow we also met with General Savchenko, the last KGB Chief of Station in Bulgaria. During our conversation he revealed the following important information:

The destruction of the Markov file would be a completely unprofessional action. Such a file would never contain either a murder plan or the names of the killers. Such things are never put down in writing. The standing KGB rule is that if a political removal is planned, it is known of by no more than three people.

Nice, clear, neat rules!

We returned to Sofia with some interesting new facts but nothing conclusive. We seemed to have encountered another dead end. Then, after a lot of telephone calls and cajoling of unwilling contacts, we managed to track down a particular woman. Before describing her though, an outline of the structure of the all-powerful KDS – the Committee for State Security – is necessary.

Throughout the years of the Communist regime, the KDS maintained a powerful public presence on the streets of Bulgaria. Though some of its officers wore uniforms, many more worked behind the scenes in plain clothes, with disguised identities.

KDS headquarters were on the 6th of September Street within the Ministry of the Interior. It had many other specialist departments in Sofia, with local command centres in every town of the nation. There were more than 30,000 regular secret police agents in Bulgaria, but there were many thousands more part-time agents and a vast network of local informers. The power and influence of the KDS spread into every area of Bulgarian life. It was organised into seven specialist departments:

Dept 1 The Intelligence Department, it was responsible for foreign espionage and the gathering of economic and military information abroad.

Dept 2 The largest section of all and responsible for counter-espionage, it monitored the activities of Bulgarian exiles throughout the world and, if it was deemed necessary, tried to control them.

Dept 3 Responsible for military counter-espionage, it had thirty subdivisions.

Dept 4 The Technical Support Department, it had its own scientific and technical laboratories and had complete access to the research departments of the universities. It was also responsible for jamming Radio Free Europe.

Dept 5 The UBO, responsible for security and vigilance, it was under the direct command of President Zhivkov. It acted as a kind of anti-post office and was responsible for intercepting mail and bugging the telephones of politically suspect citizens. It was also the praetorian guard of the Communist leadership, responsible for the physical protection of all ministers and members of the Politburo.

Dept 6 Responsible for the struggle against ideological deviation at home and enemies abroad, it acted as a kind of political police force (not surprisingly, it was one of the most feared departments). This was the department that prepared the "personal" files mentioned by General Todorov.

Dept 7 The Information and Analysis Department, responsible for gathering facts about the real situation in the country as distinct from the propaganda picture, it was the only department that knew the truth and its findings were kept absolutely confidential. Each of the departments generated its specific information files, and then sent them to the archive section in Dept 7 which also held the "personal" and "working" files.

One theory says that every department of the KDS was controlled by an adviser from the Soviet KGB, who was sometimes known as an "uncle" and who reported directly to Moscow.

About the relationship between the KDS and the KGB, General Oleg Kalugin had this to say:

Relations between us were so close that no serious action of the Ministry of the Interior (and the KDS was part of this ministry) was undertaken without our knowing about it. We knew everything that happened in Bulgaria. The Bulgarians, like true brothers and colleagues in arms, disclosed everything and we helped them whenever we could. In this sense, if we use the old terminology, we look at this as an expression of "international solidarity."

But to say that among Bulgarian citizens a whole network of KGB agents had been created, that these agents did not report to the Bulgarian authorities, that they could enter any Bulgarian institution, and that they had access to any confidential information is absolutely not true. We have always worked on the basis of full mutual confidence. There was not even one case when we acted behind the backs of our Bulgarian colleagues, effectively behind the back of the leadership of the KDS. If we had to solve some problem, we did it only with their agreement and participation. They were like members of our team, like our own agents. What did we need other agents for?

If you have in mind the KGB stations in Sofia and Varna – the officers who worked there had authority, and some power, but this was given and controlled by the Bulgarians – about twenty officers, no more. You cannot say these people represented some kind of force. They could call on any deputy minister, who would refuse a Soviet comrade. Our relationship was one of brothers-in-arms. There was no need to act behind each other's backs.

What an idyllic relationship!

Vladimir Kostov, who had also been a colonel in the KDS and had nearly lost his life thanks to those two lovebirds – the KGB and the KDS – has a different opinion of the whole relationship:

Since 1947–48 the Soviet Security Services began building their own network of agents in the East European countries, including Bulgaria. This was one of the reasons for the conflict between Stalin and Tito. Tito never tolerated KGB (then called the NKVD) activities being carried on behind his back. By contrast, the Bulgarian Party and State leadership, during the years of the Communist regime, never objected to these privileges demanded by the KGB. The same thing happened, with less enthusiasm, in the other Eastern Bloc countries. Ultimately, if the agents of the KDS were considered by the KGB as their own agents – if the security services of a small country were transformed by the security services of an enormous country into a part of its own security system – whose interests were sacrificed?

Chapter VI
Longer than the Legs of the Traitor

Up to now, some readers may have been tempted to conclude that the murder of Georgi Markov was but one exception in the otherwise blameless history of the KDS vis-à-vis the drastic and repugnant subject of killing people. Unfortunately, this is not so and in the next few passages we will recount some of the more obvious cases of removal or elimination – the KDS's euphemism for the killing of people. The information given here is all that is available and is based on conclusions of the local authorities where each incident happened. All other traces of these people in Bulgaria has long since been obliterated by the KDS.

Take the case of Suyko Srednoridski, a rocket technician:
Srednoridski left Bulgaria illegally and went temporarily to Vienna, where he applied to emigrate to the United States. While waiting for this permission, he stayed for five weeks in the home of Edith Kindel (where she and her daughter lived in a few cheaply rented rooms).

Frau Kindel recalls that one day a man in a leather jacket came to the house. He said his name was Boris and he asked for Mr Srednoridski. (Her daughter also witnessed this meeting.) Since that day the two women never saw either of the men again.

The day after Boris' visit the women entered Srednoridski's room: they found his wedding ring, a new Bulgarian-English dictionary and an old wallet with a photograph of his mother. Under the table they found a pair of old shoes (made in Bulgaria) and a pair of new Austrian boots. In the same room Frau Kindel and her daughter also found a book about America and an exercise book with words in English. The last word Srednoridski had written down was "life".

According to the Austrian police, Srednoridski would never have gone back to Bulgaria of his own accord. He left his few belongings behind. He had clearly been kidnapped. No one has ever seen him since.

Boris Arsov, strident anti-Communist:

Arsov had also left Bulgaria illegally. He was living in the Danish town of Aarhus where he started publishing his own newspaper *Levski,* in which he viciously attacked the Bulgarian regime.

In 1974 Arsov suddenly disappeared from his flat. Two months later he was brought before the Central Court in Sofia, tried and sentenced to fifteen years imprisonment. An article about the trial which appeared in the Bulgarian press quoted a statement from the court proceedings: "Arsov was playing with fire. The timely intervention of the State Security stopped his dangerous activity. This only shows that the hand of justice is longer than the legs of the traitor."

One year later Arsov was found dead in his cell. The official version was that he committed suicide, but his body was never shown to the family.

In an interview given to BBC television, a high-ranking officer from the Danish Secret Service said they had enough evidence to prove that Arsov had been kidnapped by the KDS.

Vesselina Stoynova, Ivan Kolev and Peter Nezamov, Vienna 1975:

For two years a group of Bulgarian exiles in Vienna had been successfully forging money and passports with which they helped other Bulgarians to escape from the country. In September 1975 one of the members of the group, Vesselina Stoynova, was found dead in Vienna. She had been shot twice through the head.

Hours later two other members of the group were also shot. Ivan Kolev died immediately while Peter Nezamov died from his wounds in hospital.

Another Bulgarian, Stoyan Stefanov – the leader of the group

– was identified by the Austrian police as the murderer. They mounted an extensive search but could not locate him. The only place they had not been able to search was the Bulgarian Embassy.

Two months later Stefanov appeared in Sofia. He is still alive and receives a pension every month. The reader can guess where his pension comes from.

Stefan Svredlev, former KDS agent:

Svredlev was the most important KDS agent who ever escaped to the West (excluding Vladimir Kostov who was more properly a political secret service officer). Together with his 38 year old wife, Pavlina, and his five month old son, Sergei, Svredlev crossed the Bulgarian-Greek frontier in a military jeep on the 10th of February 1975 and asked for political asylum. He had been a colonel in the KDS and Chief of State Security in the industrial city of Pernik.

To improve his chances of a bright future in the West, Svredlev had taken with him documents from strategic conferences of the Warsaw Pact and plans for dealing with opponents of the Bulgarian regime in the country and abroad: "The M-120-0050 Directive". The Greek government was not all that enthusiastic about the whole affair because of possible diplomatic difficulties with Bulgaria which his defection might raise, just at a point in time when the relations between the two countries were improving.

However, the Greek secret services were clearly impressed with the information Svredlev brought with him, so he and his family were allowed to live in Greece for eight years before they were granted political asylum in West Germany. They lived first in Munich and then in Augsburg. Meanwhile, in Bulgaria he had been tried in absentia for high treason and sentenced to death; his wife was also tried in absentia and sentenced to twenty years in prison.

In exile, though Svredlev was very active in campaigns against the Bulgarian regime, he never achieved personal success in the West. Most of the time he was employed as a construction worker while his wife applied in vain for jobs as a dentist. Svredlev turned to the West German government for help but was turned down. He carried a serious "handicap" with him: by secret service standards, he was a traitor. Furthermore, he was not very bright and so he could not be used in any intelligence capacity. After he handed over the stolen documents, he was no longer of any use to anyone. He had broken the golden rule of every secret service: never go over to the other side.

All this contributed to the strange events which happened on the 12th of September 1983. Svredlev's wife and son were going to see her mother who had taken a tourist trip to Vienna. Somewhere between Munich and Vienna, Pavlina and little Sergei disappeared.

At first, Svredlev believed that they had been kidnapped by the secret services, but then Pavlina suddenly appeared in Sofia where she accused her husband of having forced her to leave Bulgaria. Svredlev found himself caught in a vicious double web. He was considered a traitor by all secret services involved, including the Western ones. He couldn't be used as an intelligence officer by the West so he was out in the cold – like Markov, a "traitor".

Chapter VII
We Never Forgive Fugitives

Vast political changes in Bulgaria had created a new mood of hope and expectancy, and the presence in June 1991 of two Scotland Yard detectives on Bulgarian soil caused great excitement in Sofia. All the mass media were covering it, so people were, not surprisingly, deeply disappointed by the anticlimactic nature of their meetings with the Bulgarian officials for the purpose of discussing the murder of Georgi Markov. Their arrival on the 5th of June was cloaked in such secrecy that some newspapers commented that it seemed more like a top secret conference than an open murder investigation.

The Scotland Yard detectives were David Kemp and Christopher Bird. Kemp (born in 1942) had been involved in the case from the very beginning. It was he who had conducted most of the interrogations of the Bulgarian exiles working for the BBC and Radio Free Europe, and of those who knew Georgi Markov. His colleague, Bird (born in 1944) joined the investigation later, but quickly caught up with what he had missed.

The discussions between the two investigating groups concentrated mainly on new developments and on procedural questions as some legal problems existed in the event of a trial. According to Bulgarian law, evidence given on British soil cannot be used against a defendant in a Bulgarian court. Conversely, according to British law, witnesses must be assured of safety and peace of mind when being questioned. Some of the witnesses questioned in 1978 had been afraid to talk because of the threat of danger to their lives from the same source that had killed Markov.

By this time, the situation in Bulgaria had changed so much that most of the same witnesses are ready to be questioned by Bulgarian investigators and even to testify in a Bulgarian court. Some have already testified to Bulgarian investigators. One of these is Theo Lirkov, Markov's colleague at the BBC.

During the joint meetings in Sofia, the Bulgarian investigators filled the Scotland Yard detectives in on all the new facts that had been unearthed in Bulgaria, while the Yard detectives filled in any gaps in the information the Bulgarians had concerning the British investigation. For example, the British detectives had talked to the "man from Munich" who had repeatedly warned Markov.

Then, on the 8th of June, after sixteen hours of strenuous work with the Bulgarian investigators, the two British detectives left Bulgaria, apparently satisfied. They had refused to give us an interview, but promised to read our book with interest – which perhaps they should, as will be clear from the next few pages.

The chief of the Bulgarian Investigative Department, Kosta Bogatsevski, was more open and better disposed towards us, granting us a short interview. He told us about the British investigation, including the forensic results, and the results from the autopsy of Georgi Markov.

The one important result from the meetings between the British and Bulgarian investigators was the joint statement made to the effect that no evidence exists to support the theory of a shooting umbrella having been used in "the umbrella murder", as we had maintained for a year before this statement was officially declared.

Even so, with or without the umbrella, Markov had been murdered and the case remained, all these years later, unsolved.

Through a source close to the Bulgarian investigation we had full information on how it was going. The results to this date were pessimistic and were very lean in their content. All witnesses and suspects interviewed by the Bulgarian investigators had denied any involvement in the Markov murder and had given no helpful information.

The investigators had found a plan in the archives of the KDS which called for "neutralising" Georgi Markov, but the plan did not explain what was meant by the word "neutralise" and there was no further explanation or plan for the so-called neutralisation.

The details of the following events have never been published and are not known by either the Bulgarian or the British investigators, because they have not pursued the case. They lead to a solution we had suspected for a long time – a solution which not only fits with all the existing facts but also with the psychological make-up of the people and the system involved.

Now it is time to consider the testimony of the woman we tracked down after our trip to Moscow. This woman was and still is working in the Ministry of the Interior, in the archives department of the KDS. We promised never to divulge her rank or name because that would put at risk her whole career and she would be liable for prosecution on the grounds of a breach of security. We talked to her on the phone in the spring of 1991. She was very nervous but had decided to talk to us because, as she put it, she knew one of us from the TV commentary programme and she approved of what she had seen.

First, we tried to ask whether she had ever seen Markov's file, but she refused to say anything on the matter. The conversation went on for about ten minutes and at any moment we sensed that she would hang up. Finally we asked a question to which she had to answer either *yes* or *no*: "Was Markov's file among the 'personal' files?" We waited with our hearts in our mouths. After a dreadful silence she answered firmly: "No!" and hung up.

This answer meant that Markov had a "working" file!

Armed with this new ammunition, we arranged a second interview with General Vlado Todorov – the man who had supposedly destroyed Markov's file. Our second meeting with him took place in Sofia after the failed coup in the Soviet Union and Todorov was in a much different mood than previously. We told him we knew that Markov had had a "working" file, to which he replied that this made things "easier". He agreed to answer our questions:

Q Was Markov's file a "working" file?

A Yes, Markov had been recruited at the end of the fifties into the ranks of the KDS. His first tasks were to mingle among intellectuals and inform on people with ideas or actions dangerous to the Party and State. (In exchange for his small-time snitching on personal acquaintances he received favours in return; for example, it was made easier for him to get published.)

Q When Markov left for the West, did he have a mission from the KDS – was he still an agent?

A Yes, and for a while he successfully accomplished his tasks. All this was in the file.

Q Why did you say he accomplished his tasks for a while?

A Because as we found out afterwards, he had subsequently been recruited by the British Secret Service and had become a double agent. He took the whole thing as a game. He was very dangerous to us and when the British found he was a double agent, they realised he was a danger for them also.

Q Why did you take his file, and did you destroy it?

A No, I did not destroy it. I had to take it. It was my duty, it contains names of agents, codes, addresses of KGB agents who are still in the field. I could not betray them or put their lives and liberty at risk. With the situation that exists now in Bulgaria there was the danger of this file being made public. This was against the security of my country.

Q Where are these files now?

A I gave the file to my colleagues in the KGB, but I have kept enough to prove that Markov was a double agent and to prove I had nothing to do with his murder.

Q Will you come back to Bulgaria?

A Yes, and very soon. If there is a trial I will present absolute proof of my innocence and show that I acted in the interests of Bulgaria.

Q Who do you think killed Markov?

A I think he was killed by the British when they discovered he was a double agent.

This is Todorov's opinion. Still in the system, it is quite natural that he would seek to deflect attention from his own organisation by accusing the British of having killed Markov.

This ended our conversation with Vlado Todorov. He had corroborated what we ourselves had suspected for the past two years: Georgi Markov had been an agent of the KDS, and was probably a British agent as well.

This, effectively, finally answered the question of *why* the KDS had ordered the murder of Markov: he was a KDS agent who became a traitor to his homeland.

Before returning to the question of *who* killed Georgi Markov, it is necessary to address the understandably sensitive matter of Annabelle Markov's refutation of the results of our investigations. Both Annabelle Markov and her mother have often emphatically told the press that Markov could never have had any connection with the KDS. Their reason: because he never told them. The mother-in-law has even suggested that this theory was but an attempt by the Bulgarian Communists to try to defame Markov.

In answer to that, it can only be said that it was one of the authors of this book who has maintained from the beginning of our investigations that Markov was a KDS agent. The author himself has never been a member of any Communist party but has, on the contrary, been harassed and obstructed in his work as a translator and journalist – because of his cooperation with leading representatives of the Western media like the BBC,

CNN, Finnish Radio and many others – by the KDS during Zhivkov's regime.

As for the idea that Markov would have told his new and middle-class English family about his career as a spy, it takes little imagination to realise that, though Markov was never a professional in the cloak and dagger business of espionage, he certainly was not foolish enough to divulge such sensitive information to his own family members. Interesting anecdotes about exploits as a spy would hardly be the subject of family conversation over dinner or tea.

For the record, we cite two more people who spoke freely during BBC television interviews. Kyril Panov and Nikolai Khokhlov took part in the first BBC *Panorama* programme about Markov's murder, produced in 1979. The following are excerpted from those interviews.

Panov is a broadcaster and was a colleague of Georgi Markov at the BBC. He said:

> *Markov was talking in his broadcasts about things which are, so to speak, taboo in Bulgaria, things which the regime prefers not to talk about and that the public was not supposed to know. He presented Todor Zhivkov as a normal human being, as a man who might be basically a good character but who, slowly but surely, was being corrupted by the system – by power. This is, of course, something which hurts both Todor Zhivkov and the establishment as such.*

Khokhlov had been a professional killer for the KGB. During one of his missions he defected to the West and subsequently became one of the best Western experts on the KGB. Michael Cockrell of the BBC interviewed him in Britain, and asked whom he thought had killed Georgi Markov.

Khokhlov replied: "Well, of course, the intelligence services of countries that would profit from that (Markov's death) and have a vested interest in that (the death) of a person like Markov." He didn't say which countries – it could be any secret service; the important point is that secret service organisations world wide do operate in this way.

After reading what Panov had to say about Markov's broadcasts, and after considering the nature of his broadcasts on Radio Free Europe, is it credible that a cunning, down-to-earth, peasant dictator like Todor Zhivkov would risk so much simply for personal revenge, especially when half of the Bulgarian population was saying much worse things about him?

And where does Vladimir Kostov fit into all this? Ceausescu, yes, he was capable of such absurd pettiness – he wanted to blow up Radio Free Europe. He was paranoid. But Zhivkov – more calculating and politically astute – would have had to have a much more urgent reason for eliminating Markov. The revenge of wounded vanity is not a sufficient explanation.

Who then killed Georgi Markov?

Ultimately there are only two theories which fit the facts. The first maintains that the murder was committed by the British Secret Services or the CIA, when they discovered that Markov was a double agent. Before that, they shot a pellet without any poison into the body of Vladimir Kostov, with or without his agreement, so they could blame the whole affair on the KGB and the KDS, thus achieving a propaganda coup as well.

This theory is not really credible because there was no need from the West's perspective to get rid of Georgi Markov. He was neither a dangerous nor a professional agent. He could definitely be better used alive than dead. If the Western secret services were responsible for his murder, it would have required complicity by Vladimir Kostov. Yet this would have been a highly risky operation because, from the point of view of the same Western secret services (whichever might have been involved), Scotland Yard is well known for its independence and total professionalism.

Furthermore, it does not fit with the "neutralisation" plan discovered by the Bulgarian investigators, nor does it fit with

Kalugin's disclosures.

The other theory maintains that the Bulgarian secret services – the KDS and the KGB – at the request of Todor Zhivkov and with the endorsement of Yuri Andropov, appointed its own assassin, the Woodpecker, to kill Georgi Markov.

Since the beginning of the seventies there was an enormous increase in the number of people who defected from Bulgaria to the West. What was most worrying from the Bulgarian government's point of view was that these were people in whom Bulgaria had "vested interests" (to use Khokhlov's words): specialists, intellectuals, secret agents, well educated people in general. Living abroad, these successful escapees created a feeling of unrest and opposition to the regime at home. The KDS killed off some of them, kidnapped and brought back others, but the flow did not stop. People were not intimidated because these retaliatory actions were, as we have seen, carried out so secretively that the population in general did not understand the real nature of the danger.

This was the political climate at the time when the plan to kill Markov was hatched. The idea was to kill two prominent Bulgarian figures – well known to the population – who had defected to the West, as a warning to other secret service agents who might be thinking of defecting.

The two victims had to be ex-secret agents. The choice was easy: Georgi Markov and Vladimir Kostov. The method had to be flashy, like in a James Bond book, and it had to be easily discovered. Any competent pathologist would discover the pellet which was small, but not that small. The poison had to be rare but traceable.

The whole operation had to make the headlines, so that as large a part of the Bulgarian population as possible would hear and talk about the deaths. This would make it clear to everybody that the long arm of the KGB-KDS can get you anywhere.

We will probably never know who invented the plan: Todor Zhivkov, Dimitar Stoyanov, Oleg Kalugin, Vladimir Kryuchkov, Yuri Andropov – they all knew about it, but we doubt if any one of them had enough imagination to have come up with the plan.

Kalugin was trying to cover up the reason for the murder – that it was a KGB-KDS plan. A lifelong member of the "Club", he was covering up for his cronies.

The plan was put into action and succeeded by fifty per cent. Vladimir Kostov, fortunately for him, survived the attempt on his life. Yet even so, it was a surprisingly effective campaign: over the next ten years there were very few defections from Bulgaria.

In the spring of 1990 we started our journalistic investigation of the Markov murder in cooperation with a British journalist (who has asked that he remain anonymous). Our British colleague had managed to obtain a fax copy of the MI5 photograph and the name under which the man in the picture had served as a Bulgarian diplomat.

It took us about an hour to discover the address and telephone number of the man we refer to as the Woodpecker. On calling the Bulgarian Foreign Office and asking for our suspect, we were told he had retired the previous year. Next, we concocted a story about a senior school graduation anniversary gathering of Woodpecker's class (these gatherings are very popular in Bulgaria and the time of year was perfect: graduations are held on the 24th of May – the day of Bulgarian culture – and our investigations were in April 1991); we had to resort to a ruse because, at that time, Bulgaria was still labouring under the old veil of absolute secrecy.

We called the Bulgarian Foreign Office Personnel Department and gave our story with the request to obtain Woodpecker's address and telephone number as we had lost touch with him. As we expected, it went smoothly and we got our information.

Next, we called the number and found that it was indeed Woody's: his wife answered and told us that her husband had gone to buy some planks. (This was when Woodpecker got his nickname: *wood* plus the fact that we suspected he had given a deathly peck to Georgi Markov.)

We drove to Woodpecker's home, in a large block of flats on a central boulevard, flanked by a popular Sofia cinema and a big park. We waited about an hour before a well maintained Lada car stopped in front of the entrance. We knew it was Woody because of the tell-tale planks sticking out of the car window.

A fit, middle-aged man stepped out of the car. He was fifty-five to sixty years old, about five feet ten inches with a weather beaten face, steel grey straight hair with a receding hairline, hazel eyes, tight colourless lips, and a thin, elongated face. He was dressed in jeans and sports shirt, but his posture was erect and military in manner. His initials are TS.

We were with our British journalist friend and so the ensuing conversation was in English:

"TS?" we asked.

He replied: "Yes."

We tried shock tactics and asked: "What do you know about Georgi Markov?"

He took the question calmly and said: "Who's asking?"

We presented ourselves, showing our journalist ID's. He checked them with interest and answered slowly: "Before his death I didn't even know who he was; afterwards of course . . ."

"But he was a famous Bulgarian writer and the author of the most popular TV serial," we insisted.

"I dislike literature," came the pat answer.

"Have you ever worked abroad?" one of us asked.

"Yes, but during all of 1978 I was in Bulgaria," he replied.

When we analysed this conversation later, a few facts struck us as rather suspicious. First, here was a Bulgarian diplomat with a university education but who claimed he had never heard of the best known contemporary Bulgarian writer. This would be like finding a British diplomat who had never heard of Graham Greene.

Second, we have talked to many of Markov's friends and most of them could not say off-hand the precise year when he was killed – most of them remembered it was the end of the seventies – but Woody knew the very year and seemed to conclude straight off that we suspected him of murder. Although we definitely had not made any accusations, he was clearly giving us an alibi.

Third and most important: his claim to have been in Bulgaria for the whole of 1978 contradicted the evidence of the photograph made by MI5 at Heathrow airport just before Markov's murder. It is true we had only a fax copy of this picture but all three of us agreed that the man in the fax copy and Woodpecker were one and the same.

Our strange interview with Woodpecker had ended after his comments about 1978. He brushed us off by saying he was very busy and could not talk to us any more, not then or at any other time. He went to pick up his planks and as one of us was in his path, he said, "I beg your pardon" in good English but with a slight foreign accent which echoed that distant day on Waterloo Bridge.

A few days after this interview, we discovered that in 1979 TS had been made ambassador to a European country. He had also subsequently received his well situated flat, and he had managed to buy a car. These three elements indicate that Woody was a big timer by Bulgarian standards. Furthermore, the speed of his rise from Third Secretary to Ambassador is quite unprecedented and could only be explained by his having performed some "special service". Who said that murder does not pay?

Though we felt strongly that we had identified Markov's murderer, other information was still to emerge, with its own bizarre twists that cast further confusion on this troubling, unresolved case. Just when the investigations into Markov's murder seemed to have come to a complete dead end, the Bulgarian investigators found some sensational written documents in the KDS archives. This happened at the end of 1992. These documents involve a Bulgarian spy of Italian origin,

Francesco Giullino, code name "Piccadilly".

Holding Danish citizenship and speaking perfect English, Piccadilly was twenty-six years old in 1972, when he was arrested in Bulgaria and accused of drug smuggling. After a few weeks of detention he agreed to work for the "Extreme Activities" section of the First Department of the KDS. (This is the dirty works section of the Bulgarian Secret Service which does not shy away from anything, not even from murder.) His handwritten declaration of allegiance, duly signed, still exists in the archives. After his recruitment, the criminal investigation against Giullino was suspended and he left Bulgaria. He returned to Denmark and started spying for his new employers.

In 1976 Piccadilly was freed of all his tasks and was ordered to work on the operation of "neutralising" the Wanderer (the code name Markov is referred to by in the KDS archives). Between 1976 and 1978 he had a series of meetings in Bulgaria with Stoyan Savov and Vasil Kotsev, two big bosses in the Bulgarian Secret Services. Some journalists gave a lot of attention to those meetings because of the high rank of the two Bulgarians, but General Vlado Todorov told us that such meetings were standard procedure in the KDS and were aimed at improving the morale of foreign agents working for Bulgaria.

At home in Denmark, Piccadilly regularly received sums of money from a Bulgarian agent, the receipts of which exist in the archives. (The agent who carried the money is still alive but the Bulgarian investigators declined to reveal his name.) He began to visit London frequently, with the explanation that he wanted to move his business to Britain. During these visits he always rented rooms near Markov's house.

A few months before Markov's murder, Piccadilly received a sum of two thousand pounds sterling from the "Extreme Activities" section of the KDS. This is noteworthy because up to this point he had received payments only in Danish currency. After Markov's death, he continued to receive pounds sterling, US dollars and Danish kroner.

During the period around the 7th of September 1978, Piccadilly was again in London but on the 9th of September, the agent who kept contact with him was sent by General Savov to Rome. He and Piccadilly were to pass by each other on a prearranged street so that Giullino, by holding his newspaper in a certain way, could signal whether the operation against Markov had been executed or not.

After 1978 Piccadilly visited Bulgaria many times, while still living in Copenhagen where he was for some time the owner of a shop for old paintings and antiques, and the possessor of two counterfeit passports.

In November 1992 the Bulgarian investigators sent copies of the documents concerning Francesco Giullino to Scotland yard, expecting great interest and a breakthrough in the case. Piccadilly was questioned by the Danish police at the request of Scotland Yard. He admitted his spying activities, but categorically denied the accusations of being involved in Markov's murder. It seems that Scotland Yard did not take the recent Bulgarian discoveries very seriously because, after being questioned for six hours, Piccadilly was released. On the 25th of June 1993 he sold all his properties in Copenhagen and left the country. According to some sources, he now lives in Hungary. He is 47 years old, balding and of average height. In addition to his excellent English, he speaks good Bulgarian and some French,

Not surprisingly, neither the Bulgarian authorities nor the press were very happy about the way in which the British and Danish police acted in this case. For the first time since the democratic changes in Bulgaria, both the press and the authorities criticised Scotland Yard and voiced the opinion that there might be something fishy in the whole Markov case.

The director of the national Investigative Services, Colonel Any Kruleva publicly said she considered the actions taken by the British and Danish police as more of a warning to Giullino to disappear than as a proper investigation. Here are Any Kruleva's words:

> *The unprofessional actions of the British and Danish secret services on this question make me suspect that Georgi Markov's murder might have been caused by other services. It could be the KDS, it could be the KGB, but it could also be some other secret*

service. Scotland Yard admits it cannot get to the bottom of all secrets on British soil. In all these years they have given very little to the press. My suspicions will exist until I see the end of this case.

These are very strong words from the official Bulgarian authorities which up to this point had been ready to accept that the KDS had killed Markov because he had offended Zhivkov.

How does Francesco Giullino fit into the whole story? Let us first look into the theory that he was Markov's murderer. This is highly unlikely because, first of all, he was a foreigner. We talked to many ex-KDS agents and they all agreed that if there was a decision to kill somebody, the task would have been given to a Bulgarian agent – a foreigner would be too risky and would open the possibility of some kind of blackmail.

Secondly, according to the documents found in the KDS archives, Piccadilly was in London on the day when the attempt was made on Vladimir Kostov's life was made. To have two murderers using the same method is a bit far fetched.

Thirdly, if Giullino had been recruited because of his drug smuggling activities – which from the KDS point of view was small-time – it would mean the KDS had been using a dubious criminal for a very sensitive and dangerous operation.

Another more likely possibility is that Piccadilly was only the finger man who studied Markov's daily routine and helped in the preparation of the murder while the murder itself was committed by someone else (the most likely suspect still being Woodpecker). In this case, Giullino would also have been the contact person who gave the signal of success on the street in Rome, while the actual murderer was rapidly covering his tracks.

But why did Scotland Yard and the Danish police act in such a strange manner when given the information by the Bulgarian investigators? Even if Piccadilly had had nothing to do with the Markov murder, he was a self-admitted spy and there was enough evidence against him for the Danish authorities to have prosecuted him.

Two explanations come to mind. The first one is that Scotland Yard was satisfied because they had enough facts to show that

Giullino had had nothing to do with the Markov murder, while the Danish authorities were not interested in prosecuting an ex-spy for a country which is no longer an enemy and thereby preferred to let bygones be bygones.

The second one is more sinister. According to this theory, Francesco Giullino was a double (or triple) agent working for the Bulgarian KDS and for the British and Danish secret services as well. This is not out of character for a criminal like Piccadilly. In this case, it would have been embarrassing to prosecute him for his work for the KDS, so the only solution would be to let him go.

On the other hand, it may be that the British authorities did not feel, even with the information provided by the Bulgarians, that they had sufficient information to satisfy a Danish court that Giullino should be extradited to England. For the same reason, the Danish police may have felt they did not have sufficient information to hold Giullino for a longer period. It may also be that Giullino did not genuinely have Danish nationality and was in fact ordered to leave that country, as the strongest sanction which the Danish police could legitimately impose.

Other theories are possible, but we are not going to discuss them because we do not have facts to substantiate them. The important thing is that suddenly Scotland Yard was in a difficult position and was being accused by the Bulgarian investigators of inactivity, at the least. This led to the theatrical arrest of ex-KGB General Oleg Kalugin at London's Heathrow Airport in November 1993 by Scotland Yard.

This arrest may have achieved two things. First, it showed some activity by Scotland yard, although Kalugin had already been telling the world about his involvement in the Markov murder for about a year and a half. Secondly, it could have acted as a warning to other retired spies not to enhance their incomes by divulging half-truths and half-inventions about their former employers to the press. Naturally, at this time Kalugin denied any involvement in the Markov operation and Scotland Yard had to free him when the Russian Embassy protested.

Scotland Yard expressed the will to interview other KGB officers pointed out by Kalugin, like General Golubev. If this were done, however, the suspects would deny their involvement and that would be the end of this whole chapter of the Markov mystery.

Georgi Markov's love of gambling and his sense of adventure led him into a game which is only for "professionals" – people with marble heads, not writers. Markov never fully understood the cardinal rule of all secret service organisations: once a member of the "Club", always a member. The same rules apply to the Mafia. Though Markov may not have originally perceived this, as time went on his writer's instinct told him and he sensed his entrapment.

In a scene from one of his plays written in London after his defection, this sense of premonition glowers through:

Policeman: *I stopped for a moment and he disappeared. Made for the forest . . .*

Man: *What? He escaped?*

Policeman: *No one manages to escape from us, sir. I went after him and caught him like a lamb. I handcuffed him and took him to the barracks.*

Man: *What will happen to him?*

Policeman: *If he had not tried to escape, he would have saved his skin. Now there will be a court martial and they will shoot him.*

Man: *What is so bad in trying to escape?*

Policeman: *We should never show any mercy.*

Man: *But maybe he was just frightened?*

Policeman: *That has nothing to do with the case. The important thing is he tried to escape, to be free. We never forgive fugitives. We never forgive.*

Georgi Markov was killed by the KDS and the KGB. His bid for freedom was nipped in the bud during the cold war, when two political systems were struggling to destroy each other. His actual killer, whom we have identified as TS, was a Bulgarian diplomat and a KDS agent, and now, ironically, he lives as a free citizen in Sofia.

Although the Soviet Union as we knew and feared it, along with its satellite nations with their Communist regimes, has disintegrated and is past history, the secret service organisations still exist and will go on into the foreseeable future. Even now the KGB is being reorganised under Vadim Bakatin and Oleg Kalugin. It will be staffed with the same old "Club" members, because they are professionals and because state "security" remains top priority, no matter who is in power.

In an interview for CNN, Vadim Bakatin said the KGB will exist as long as the CIA exists. For once the world is not divided into two awesome and obviously opposing political camps, but the struggle is unabated and the security services of the more powerful nations continue to dictate to the weaker countries.

This book presents a brief glimpse of two of the most fearsome security organisations of the world, the KGB and the KDS. But these are neither the only ones nor categorically the most fearsome: the French Secret Service, the South African Secret Service, the Israeli Secret Service (Mossad), MI5, and especially the CIA – none is any less formidable.

The members of these "Clubs" respect neither laws nor constitutions nor citizens' rights. They commit horrific crimes and get off scot-free – like the murderers of Georgi Markov, like countless more, some whose names we know and those whose names we will never know. Often these organisations create enemies in order to justify their own existence and the enormous funds they require to carry out their "work". The news is full of these tales: Irangate, the Iraqi Supergun. The list is sadly endless.

Is it possible to imagine a world without secret service organisations? We wish we could, but it seems too good to be true.

POSTSCRIPT

The Markov case continues to make news around the world. The following is an extract from a Reuters report published in *The Daily Telegraph* on the 7th of January 1992:

GENERAL IN MARKOV CASE IS FOUND DEAD

A Bulgarian general linked to the unsolved murder of the exiled dissident Georgi Markov has been found dead, police said in Sofia.

Mr Leonid Katzamunski said it was not clear if General Stoyan Savov, former Deputy Interior Minister, had been murdered or if he had committed suicide.

His body was found near his birthplace, Lesichevo, about 60 miles south west of Sofia.

Mr Markov, a writer who worked for the BBC, died in 1978 after feeling a sharp jab in the leg as he waited at a London bus stop. A pellet of the poison ricin was later found in his thigh, apparently injected with an umbrella tip.

General Savov and the former Bulgarian intelligence chief, General Vladimir Todorov, had been charged with removing Markov's file from state archives. Their trial was to start tomorrow.

General Savov had earlier said he would give details of the case in court.

Though to date Markov's murder remains officially unsolved, it still bursts into the news from time to time. The brief arrest of Oleg Kalugin in November 1993 by Scotland Yard, on charges pertaining to this case, brought Markov's name and story back into the minds of British citizens and resulted in considerable renewed press and media coverage. Indeed, even in the House of Commons one Member of Parliament raised the question: "Why hasn't the murder of Georgi Markov been solved?"

Appendices

Appendix A

Notes: Vladimir Kryuchkov, Vladimir Kostov and Yanko Stefanov

Vladimir Kryuchkov was born in 1924 in the city of Volgograd. He attended law school and then the post-graduate diplomatic school of the Ministry of Foreign Affairs of the USSR. He started working for the KGB in 1967. He was First Deputy Chairman of the KGB from 1978 to 1988, when he became Chairman of the KGB. From 1989 to 1990 he was a member of the Politburo of the Central Committee of the Soviet Communist Party.

Kryuchkov was considered the brain behind the attempted coup against Gorbachev in August 1991 and is probably correctly called the "Grey Cardinal". This fat-cheeked, 69 year old man is referred by Western journalists as a typical "Homo Sovieticus". A colourful personality, he is a hard-drinking man with a nostalgic feeling for the old regime. He is now being prosecuted for his part in the failed coup, but he is a member of the "Club" and so it is belief of the authors of this book that he will never go to prison.

Vladimir Kostov maintains that, in an article published in Bulgaria on the 26th of March 1991, the file on Markov was not destroyed and that it was, on the contrary, deposited with the KGB. He is convinced the file contains sensitive material related to Markov's activities.

Yanko Stefanov, the ex-Chief of the KDS in Varna (the biggest port city in Bulgaria) and a Bulgarian agent in London during the period 1960-1964, maintains that Markov worked for three intelligence services, including the KDS. He said he knows this because of his job, but he declines to offer any proof.

Appendix B

The opening up of society in Bulgaria under Khrushchev

During the Khrushchev era in the Soviet Union the ideological ice covering Russia started to melt a little and that led to the publication of Solzhenitsyn's book *One Day in the Life Ivan Denysovich,* the books by Vassily Arkanov and other modern Russian authors. This climate was also felt in Bulgaria and one of the "new wave" authors was Georgi Markov. But after Brezhnev's ascension to power and the destruction of the "Prague Spring", icy winds once again blew over Eastern Europe. Only a few intellectuals in Bulgaria had the courage to openly protest and they were immediately crushed. Some went to prison, others lost their jobs, some left the country. Some Bulgarian authors say that the crushing of the "Prague Spring" and the reaction in Bulgaria led to Markov's decision to emigrate.

Appendix C

Note on KGB laboratories

Going back to its earliest days – when it was known as the Chekha – the KGB had different laboratories which dealt with all technical and scientific aspects of spying and surveillance. Some of the best scientists and technicians of the Soviet Union worked for the KGB. The laboratories were known by different numbers and dealt with things like secret weapons, forgeries, electronic surveillance devices, chemical and biological research, forensics, psychiatry and psychology. Nothing was left out. But then, this is true of all big state security organisations like the CIA, Mossad, MI5 and MI6.

Appendix D

Ricin articles

Unlike the sinister and deadly use of ricin by the KGB, current research in Britain and America is studying the applicability of ricin to cancer treatment and the development of healthier strains of agricultural plants.

The cover of this book shows how ricin is composed of two separate protein molecules or "chains". The B chain, shown in blue, binds to (human) cells. By doing this, it helps the red A chain get into those cells. Once inside the cells, the A chain attacks the machinery used by cells to make their own proteins. These machines are called ribosomes. What makes ricin potentially so nasty is that the A chain is an enzyme of which only one chain can kill thousands of ribosomes. In the picture there are little skeletal models on either end of the B chain "dumbbell". These are sugar representations and they mark where ricin grabs onto cells. There is a yellow skeleton near the centre of the red A chain. This marks the "mouth" – or active site – of the enzyme.

Following are extracts from three research articles about ricin, included here by permission of Jon D Robertus.

Ricin is a heterodimeric protein isolated from the seeds of the castor plant, *Ricinus communis* [and] is an extraordinarily toxic molecule. It binds eurcaryotic cell surfaces via the RTB lectin action and enters the cell during endocytosis. RTA escapes from the endosome by an unknown mechanism; in the cytoplasm it attacks ribosomes, removing a specific adenine base from rRNA and thereby inhibiting protein synthesis.

Ricin is a common component of immuno-toxins targeted against tumor cells or in the treatment of graft versus host disease. Trichosanthin has been used in China since antiquity as an abortifacient; more recently, it has been shown to inhibit replication of HIV-1 in cultured cells. Other RIPs are currently being tested for activity against AIDS-infected cells. RIP genes might also be introduced into agriculturally significant plants to eliminate virus sensitivity.

Ricin toxin B-chain (RTB) is the sugar binding moiety of the cytotoxic plant protein ricin. It is linked to the A-chain (RTA) by a disulfide bond. RTB binds reversibly to galactose residues presented by cell surface glycopeptides and glycolipids and facilitates uptake of whole ricin by endocytosis. Following reduction of the disulfide bond RTA is released into the cytoplasm, where its action as an N-glycosidase inactivates cellular ribosomes, often resulting in cell death...

Several research groups have investigated the sugar binding properties of ricin using a variety of methods.

References

For readers wishing to know more about the culturally interwoven history of Bulgaria, The Hon Sir Steven Runciman's *History of the First Bulgarian Empire* is still considered to be the single best book on the subject, in spite of having been written 63 years ago and wanting, therefore, modern up-dating. His own view is that the early chapters ought to be re-written to include archaeological evidence that was not available to him when he wrote in 1930. However, as a sign of their respect and appreciation for the noteable scholarship of Sir Steven's book, the Bulgarian government recently translated and published his book in Bulgaria.

For the reader wishing to have a more detailed understanding of the history and complexities of secret service systems, the following are a few suggestions with which to begin:

- Agee, Philip, *Inside the Company: CIA Diary* (Stonehill, 1975)

- Andrew, Christopher, *Secret Service: The Making of the British Intelligence Community* (Heinemann, 1985)

- Andrew, Christopher, and Gordievsky, Oleg, *KGB: The Inside Story (of its Foreign Operations from Lenin to Gorbachev)* (Hodder & Stoughton, 1990)

- Barron, John, *KGB Today: The Hidden Hand* (Hodder & Stoughton, 1983)

- CIA, *The Rote Kapelle: The CIA's History of Soviet Intelligence and Espionage Networks in Western Europe, 1936-1945* (University Publications of America, 1979)

- Deriabin, Peter, and Bagley, TH, *The KGB: Masters of the Soviet Union* (Hippocrene, 1990)

- Dulles, Allen, *The Craft of Intelligence* (Harper & Row, 1968)

- Khokhlov, Nikolai, *In the Name of Conscience* (McKay, 1959)
- Kuzichkin, Vladimir, *Inside the KGB* (André Deutsch, 1990)
- Leggett, George, *The Cheka: Lenin's Political Police* (OUP, 1981)
- Levchenko, Stanislav, *On the Wrong Side* (Pergamon-Brassey, 1988)
- Lonsdale, Gordon, *Spy* (Neville Spearman, 1965)
- Orlov, Alexander, *The Secret History of Stalin's Crimes* (Random House, 1953)
- Orlov, Alexander, *Handbook of Intelligence and Guerrilla Warfare* (University of Michigan Press, 1963)
- Philby, Kim, *My Silent War* (McGibbon & Kee, 1968)
- Ranelagh, *CIA a history* (BBC Books, 1992)
- Romerstein, Herbert, and Levchenko, Stanislav, *The KGB against the 'Main Enemy'* (Lexington, 1989)
- Tsarev, Oleg, and Costello, John, *Deadly Illusions* (Random Century, 1993)
- West, Nigel, *The Illegals: The Double Lives of the Cold War's Most Secret Agents* (Hodder & Stoughton, 1993)
- West, Nigel, *The Friends: Britain's Post-War Secret Intelligence Operations* (Weidenfeld & Nicolson, 1992)
- Wright, Peter, *Spycatcher* (Viking, 1987)

Index

Andrew, Christopher: 47-50
Andropov, Yuri: 34, 53-55, 61, 63-64, 81-82
Arkanov, Vassily: 96
Arsov, Boris: 71
Bakatin, Vadim: 90
Belyaev, Alexander: 57
Bereanu, Vladimir: 4, 55-56, 58
Beria, Lavrenty: 54
Bird, Christopher: 74-75
Blunt, Sir Anthony: 47
Bogatsevski, Kosta: 75
Brezhnev, Leonid: 34, 39, 48, 96
Burgess, Guy: 47
Cairncross, John: 47
Carlos: 52
Castro, Fidel: 39
Ceausescu, Nicolae: 34, 39, 80
Chebrikov, Viktor: 54
Chernenko: 34
Cockrell, Michael: 79
Danov, Rumen: 55, 57
Dubcek, Alexander: 48
Fyodorov, Vladilen: 64
Gall, Dr David: 18-19
Genadiev: 43
Geshakov, Asen: 58-59
Giullino, Francesco *(Piccadilly):* 85-88
Golubev, Sergei Michaylovich: 53-55, 88
Gorbachev, Mikhail: 34-35, 47, 52, 95
Gordievsky, Oleg: 47-50, 56, 61

HD: 33, 40-44
Hodzha, Enver: 39
Hyena: 41-44
Jaruzelski, General Zoychek: 48
Jelev, Jelyo: 55, 64
Kalugin, Oleg Danailovich: 6, 50-62, 68-69, 81-82, 88, 90, 93
Karayotov, Bogdan: 31
Katzamunski, Leonid: 93
Kemp, David: 74-75
Khokhlov, Nikolai: 79-81
Khrushchev, Nikita: 34, 37, 39, 96
Kim Il Sung: 39
Kindel, Edith: 70
King Boris: 39
King Ferdinand: 39
King Simeon: 8
Kolev, Ivan: 71
Kostov, Vladimir: 21-25, 29, 31, 55-56, 61, 69, 72, 80-82, 87, 95
Kotsev, General Vasil: 54, 64, 85
Kruleva, Colonel Any: 86
Kryuchkov, Vladimir: 50, 53, 61-62, 81, 95, *(The Grey Cardinal):* 95
Lenin, Vladimir Ilych: 39, 47
Lina: 41-42
Lirkov, Theo: 14, 18, 75
Maclean, Donald: 47
Markov, Annabelle: 15-16, 28, 78-79
Markov, Georgi, *(Gosho):* 27, *(Jerry):* 42-43, *(The Wanderer):* 85
Markov, Nikola: 15-16, 25, *(Kolyo):* 26-28
Nezamov, Peter: 71
Nixon, Richard: 35, 49
Orlov, Alexander: 6
Ormankov, Yordan: 44-45

Panov, Kyril: 79-80
Philby, Kim: 47
Pope John Paul II: 35
Savchenko, General Ivan Tichohovich: 62-63, 66
Savov, Deputy Minister Stoyan: 64-65, 85-86, 93
Semerdjiev, General Athanos: 63-64
Serkedjieva, General Nanka: 64
Solzhenitsyn, Alexander: 96
Simeonov, Vladimir: 17-19, 25
Srednoridski, Suyko: 70-71
Stalin, Joseph: 37, 39, 54, 69
Stefanov, Stoyan: 71-72
Stefanov, Yanko: 95
Stolyova, Vesselina: 71
Stoyanov, Dimitar: 53, 60-61, 63, 65, 81
Svredlev, Pavlina: 72-73
Svredlev, Stefan: 72-73
TS: 83-84, 90
Tito, Marshall Iosip Bros: 39, 69
Todorov, Kalin: 4
Todorov, Stanko: 62
Todorov, General Vladimir (Vlado): 64-66, 68, 76-78, 85, 93
Ulbricht, Walter: 39
Usatov, Deputy General: 53
Vejinova, Nina: 45
Vejinov, Pavel: 45
Woodpecker: 31, 61, 81-84, 87
Yakovlev, Egor: 35
Zhivkov, Todor: 29-30, 34-39, 53, 56, 58-61, 67, 79-81, 86
  (Chaika): 36